THE
Awesome
Power
OF THE
Healing
Thought

THE Awesome Power OF THE Healing Thought

John W. Drakeford

Broadman Press
Nashville, Tennessee

Dewey Decimal Classification: 158

Subject heading: PSYCHOLOGY, APPLIED

Library of Congress Catalog Card Number: 80-70915

Printed in the United States of America

Contents

Fix your thoughts on what is true

and good and right.

Think about things that are pure

and lovely, and

Dwell on the fine, good things

in others.

Think about all you can praise

God for and be glad about.

Philippians 4:8, TLB

Introduction:
The Time Bomb Within

The book is not really a book at all, it's a political pamphlet, a mere sixty pages long, but in terms of its influence this little volume written by Karl Marx and Frederick Engels must be one of the most significant documents ever penned. Titled *The Communist Manifesto,* it states as its basic premise, "We openly declare that our ends can only be obtained by the forcible overthrow of all existing conditions."[1] This one basic idea has been responsible for death, terror, destruction, the overthrow of governments, uprooting great hosts of people from their hearth and home, creating totalitarian societies, and changing the political map of the world. This one-sentence statement is a graphic illustration of the power of a thought or an idea.

Fortunately, thoughts have other creative possibilities. The Bible has laid down the basic principle, significantly in the book of Proverbs, a writing given over to the subject of wisdom, in a statement which reads, "As [a man] thinketh in his heart, so is he" (Prov. 23:7). What we think determines what we become. Our focus in this book will be on the possibility of the tremendous influence of ideas, particularly the way that thoughts can affect our bodies and we will zero in on one particular concept—the healing thought. There never was a time more appropriate for exploring some new healing potentialities for an ailing humanity faced with some new destructive threats.

It had been a hectic trip down the San Bernardino Valley from the mountain ranch following an enjoyable weekend. Mistiming the length of the journey, our driver had put the hammer down, and when at last I checked in at the air terminal and boarded the plane, I collapsed into my seat with a sigh of relief and gratitude that I was still in the land of the living, though in an exhausted condition. I would rest on the way back and leave the responsibility for the next three hours in the pilot's hands.

"Ladies and gentlemen," a voice came over the PA system, calling me back from the mists of slumberland, "please gather all the articles you brought on board the plane and stand in the aisle of the aircraft. We are going to disembark. There is no need for panic. We have had a bomb scare. A telephone caller claims there is a bomb aboard our plane. It is probably just a scare, but we are taking no chances. We will search the aircraft. As you leave the plane please do not speak to or pass objects to anybody. Proceed down the stairs to the bus drawn up alongside."

A silence settled over the group as we quietly moved off the plane and down to the waiting bus in which we drove to an unused building. The following hours were frustrating as airline employees arrived with our luggage and FBI agents interrogated each passenger about possibilities of vengeance seekers, and then politely requested each to open his luggage for examination.

No bomb was found in either plane or luggage but the prolonged experience put many nerves on edge. Whispered conferences, speculation, and rumor characterized the tedious hours that followed. Once permission was given, the beleagured passengers rushed to the telephones to call and explain their situation to distant waiting friends and relatives. However, throughout the entire ordeal, no one complained. If there were the slightest possibility of a bomb in the aircraft, we wanted it found.

What a contrast this makes with the attitude of many people to the time bomb many of us have within our bodies today. Perhaps in part because the threat lacks the drama of the airplane situation, one of the most threatening diseases today is hypertension, called the "silent killer." Because it may be without symptoms, people are remarkably casual about the danger of such a condition in our bodies. One hypertensive, asked how high his blood pressure was, responded, "If I don't have it taken I won't know and have to worry about it." This illness arising primarily from stress is potentially ready to blow us apart but we remain remarkably casual in our attitudes toward this possibility.

My experience with the bomb threat had a sequel. When at last, after some six or seven hours of searching and questioning, we finally boarded the plane, the airline resorted to its universal palliative—drinks on the house. As the liquor flowed, it washed away passengers' anxiety and the mood of the group underwent a not-so-subtle change. The people who had been so thoughtful and apprehensive earlier, abandoned their fears and in a relatively short time the plane began to rock with the loud conversation and boisterous activities of the liquor lubricated passengers.

Which is not so different from the multitude of palliatives offered to us in our society today. Particularly those of the chemical variety. It has been said that the universal counsel today is, "Sit still and take a pill." No counsel could be worse. Passivity will not do it. Although we are concentrating on a thought, we must see it is not a thought which is an end in itself, it is an action thought.

We are concentrating on a certain type of thought—a healing thought. Later we will make a distinction between two forms of thought, the fantasy and the vision. The fantasy is an end in itself; it remains a thought, a consoling image that brings unreal comfort to the subject. The vision by way of contrast calls for action. Years ago a great thinker wrote an article with the title, "Ideas That Have Used Me," indicating the way in which he felt certain ideas had pushed him pell-mell into situations he would normally have avoided. These ideas that motivate us are what we call the vision. The vision has a propensity for translating itself into action. Once again the Bible states a principle. Jesus said it, "Ye have heard that it was said by them of old time, Thou shalt not commit adultery: But I say unto you, That whosoever looketh on a woman to lust after her hath committed adultery with her already in his heart" (Matt. 5:27-28). The thought had such a tremendous potential that it would almost inevitably be translated into action.

In this book we will be talking about meditation and relaxation. You will be taught some ways you can learn to release the tension from your body. If you follow the plan, there will be at least twenty minutes of your day in which you will do absolutely nothing and feel good about it. But if you feel this is essentially a treatise on being still, you have missed it. Even relaxation and meditation are *action*. You will not drift into them. You must make a deliberate decision to undertake a program of meditation and relaxation. It is one of the many actions you are going to learn to undertake.

Having completed your relaxation-meditation routine, you are going to get up and get going—move on out.

The increased affluence and advanced technology in our society today mean that the average person is faced with an astounding array of choices. An American today is like a child entering a well-stocked candy store and being told he can have whatever he wishes to take. The problem is not the availability of all the creature comforts but the choice that must be made.

One writer recently pointed out that in 1975, while the USA spent $22 billion to buy alcohol, $12 billion to purchase tobacco, only $400 million were spent for cancer research. She remarks, "There is something distasteful in the sight of a highly developed society being forced to divert great resources . . . to the cure of its own self-inflicted diseases. We can characterize these as diseases of choice."[2]

"Diseases of choice" is a striking phrase which immediately raises the issue of the possibility for people having life and health by choice. There are potentialities in the human body and mind that are virtually untouched. Readers of this book will have to decide if they want to develop some of the capacities within themselves by taking a decisive action. Knowles warns us, "We do not die as often as we kill ourselves."[3] This book will lay a constant emphasis on choosing life. One important step in this will be taking a decisive action.

In one clinic[4] which works with cancer patients in a terminal condition, one question the therapists ask the patients is, "What benefits is this illness bringing you?" Benefit? A terminal illness? Surprisingly, people who are ill will often discover this sickness is bringing them some gain. Sometimes the benefit is attention, the drama of surgery, special pampering from hitherto indifferent family members or friends. Some doctors have not been slow to capitalize on this human propensity. At one hospital a particular doctor's patients were constantly relating stories of the way in which the doctor caught them in the nick of time and by his miraculous surgery plucked them from the jaws of death.

In many ways the welfare systems of our nation have encouraged the idea that it is more profitable to be sick than to be well. A case in England has dramatized the situation.[5] Two London doctors spent four years investigating the medical history of one Stewart McIlroy who was admitted as a patient to sixty-eight different hospitals on at least 207 occasions and had been x-rayed and blood-tested thousands of times. His spine was punctured on at least forty-eight occasions for spinal fluid and he sported an abdomen that was crisscrossed with scars left by the incisions of exploratory operations. With a flair for fabrication, McIlroy changed his name twenty-two times (he was traced by the clinical records of his scars) and became a past master at the art of using medical jargon to describe his symptoms. McIlroy's medical costs could be as high as $1,000,000, but of course he didn't pay, with the major proportion of the bill footed by Britain's medical health service. Mr. McIlroy just sat back and enjoyed his suffering.

There is also the idea that certain germs have invaded the human body so the victim is in no way to blame for what has happened to him. Holistic medicine comes with another message. As one practitioner says it, "The key principle underlying the entire holistic health concept is responsibility."[6] A person's health comes largely from what he does with his body and with his thoughts.

The present situation in our segmented approach to medicine has compounded the difficulties in the continuing battle against disease. During the so-called "Battle of Britain" the success or failure of the German bombing came more and more to depend upon electronics. Realizing the Royal Air

Force could not handle the waves of night bombers over the British Isles, countermeasures focused on the Radio Guidance System utilized by the night raiders. The British efforts at confusing the radio beams were achieving considerable success when the Germans came up with a new, sophisticated electronic guidance device known as the "X Apparatus." To handle this new threat it was essential that the British get their hands upon a plane with the "X Apparatus" intact. Without a chance to examine this equipment, the initiative in the Battle of Britain lay with the Germans.

Then came a golden opportunity to acquire this priceless treasure. A German Heinkle Bomber equipped with the "X Apparatus" made a forced landing on a British beach between the high and low watermark. An almost incredible example of interservice rivalry followed. The Army had arrived first at the scene and the troops were preparing to drag the plane to higher land. Suddenly a naval vessel appeared and its commanding officer claimed that because the plane was in the water it belonged to the Navy. The crew attached a rope to the machine and the vessel proceeded to tow it into the harbor. The rope suddenly snapped and the plane sank. Although the plane and the highly-prized "X Apparatus" were later salvaged, it took ten precious days to clean the sand out of the equipment so that it could be thoroughly examined.

The trend toward specialization in medicine has meant a closer focusing on very minute functionings of the body. A man who went to an internist was told he would need to go to a surgeon and a dermatologist. The patient lamented the ever-increasing specialization of medicine and the internist smilingly remarked, "If that knot on your little finger bothers you, you may have to see a little finger doctor."

One of the most encouraging developments in medicine today has been the emergence of holistic medicine. The word *holistic* comes from the Greek word *holos,* literally meaning, "whole." One of the most capable advocates of this approach has described the underlying concept:

"Fundamental to holistic medicine is the recognition that each state of health and disease requires a consideration of all contributing factors: psychological, psychosocial, environmental, and spiritual."[7] This latter factor has frequently been overlooked, despite the traditional relationship between religion and medicine.

In this book we will focus on the contribution of the spirit to the body and the way in which spiritual forces can be used to attain the condition that God wants us to enjoy in living our lives.

Part I
The Dilemma

1
An Age of Stress

Advertising creates the appetite upon which American business feeds. Without Madison Avenue, Wall Street would be sadly handicapped. Realizing the importance of advertising, twenty-five years ago the highly respected magazine, *Saturday Review,* instituted an award for advertising which it referred to as "a new frontier in communication." The magazine conceived of advertisers using print "as an instrument to secure the public interest along with a company's private interest." One of the winners in the twenty-fifth anniversary contest held in 1979 was the Liberty National Life Insurance Company. The award-winning advertisement proclaimed, "Stress can squeeze years off your life if you don't know how to handle it."[1] It may be that advertising is coming of age and turning its attention not only to the appetites of our society but also to its ills. Significantly the award-winning advertisement emphasizes the importance of controlling stress.

The advertisement's use of "squeeze" conjured up visions of an experience in Canada traveling along a highway to a place where road repairs caused it to narrow. The road sign read, "Squeeze In." I roared with laughter at the time when I saw it but that advertisement reminded me life is like a long highway and we are constantly being forced to make adaptations and "squeeze in."

A company, concerned about the morale of its top executives, called in a management consultant organization. The report of the results of this consultation stunned them. Twenty-one of the twenty-two man executive committee were suffering from such illnesses as ulcers, high blood pressure, or depression, and their report pointed to one culprit—stress.

This company is not alone. Stress is taking its toll on the American business world. The American Heart Association estimates heart-related diseases cost industry $23.7 million in 1975 and many of these were stress-related. The president of an organization developing programs to cope with stress has estimated that the total cost of stress to industry is over $100 billion a year.

It has long been known that certain higher level positions in industry and types of occupations, such as air traffic controllers, have been vulnerable to stress but new evidence is showing that stress has "downward mobility." One study carried on by the National Institute for Occupational Safety and Health in Tennessee discovered the jobs which induced the most stress in workers included such unlikely occupations as laborer, secretary, waitress, machine operator, miner, inspector, and painter. Other high stress jobs included hairdresser, meat cutter, plumber, railroad switchman, and warehouse worker. On this study the inescapable conclusion was that stress has abandoned its business suit and buttondown shirt collar for the blue collar of men and pink collar of women. Stress is no longer the privileged possession of the executive and professional classes.

Searching to find out what these jobs did to people, the same researchers came out with a list of 174 diseases which they stated were stress-related. These health problems spread from heart disease, ulcers, and hypertension to alcoholism,

THE STRESS FACTOR[2]

MOST STRESS JOBS	LOW STRESS JOBS
Laborer	Clothing Sewer
Secretary	Checker, Examiner
Inspector	Stock Handler
Clinical Lab	Craft Worker
Technician	Maid
Office Manager	Farm Laborer
Foreman	Heavy-equipment
Manager/Admini-	Operator
strator	Freight Handler
Waitress/Waiter	Child-care Worker
Machine Operator	Package Wrapper
Farm Owner	College Professor
Miner	Personnel Worker
Painter	

HIGH STRESS JOBS

Bank Teller	Plumber
Clergyman	Policeman
Computer	Practical Nurse
Programmer	Public-Relations
Dental Assistant	Person
Electrician	Railroad Switchman
Fireman	Registered Nurse
Guard/Watchman	Sales Manager
Hairdresser	Sales Representative
Health Aide	Social Worker
Health Technician	Structural-metal
Machinist	Worker
Meatcutter	Teacher's Aide
Mechanic	Telephone Operator
Musician	Warehouse Worker
Nurses' Aide	

depression and anxiety, and a variety of phobias.

And, lest you get the idea the best thing to do is to flee the big city, before you turn in your resignation, sell your house, pack your goods, and head for peaceful pastoral New England, stop and consider two studies carried out by the Vermont Heart Association.[3] This Association screened 1,600 men between the ages of twenty and sixty-four as part of a hypertension educational program. Their results showed that Vermonters could certainly use some education concerning hypertension as the rate of hypertension was twice the national 13 percent average.

Some other startling information came to light. Statistics showed that part of the country has a high suicide rate. While the national suicide average is 12.5 per 100,000, in New Hampshire it was 19.3 per 100,000, and in Maine 17.9, but in beautiful, peaceful Vermont it was the highest in the nation, with suicides at the rate of 21.4 deaths per 100,000.

What looks like beautiful, restful countryside where life can be lived in pastoral quietness brings its own peculiar stresses. A representative of the Vermont Heart Association pointed out that although the snow scenes looked pretty on postcards, when it came to living in Vermont life can be tough. Little industry locates there. Many people living in the rural areas are underpaid. Therefore, trying to live on minimum wages in snow areas takes its toll. A further complication is the self-image of the hardy Yankee to whom seeking help with emotional problems seems like an indication of weakness. All of these mount up to the apparently contradictory fact of pastoral stress.

Every age of life brings its own set of distinctive stressors. The American college scene would seem to be a glorious retreat from a chaotic world. Parents, the Federal government, or some other benefactor footing the bill; girls proving they are liberated, boys and girls living and playing in coed dorms and engaged in the serious academic pursuits of courses in organic gardening, round dancing, scuba diving, backpacking, and the theory of football; all moving to a climactic conclusion which lead to a pass-fail grade or the opportunity to drop the course at will.

It turns out there is another side to academe. Many of the support systems of yesterday's large families have been lost as, too, has the strange camaraderie that emerged in the late 60s when groups committed themselves to highly idealistic causes, stirring up and encouraging each other in a united front against the establishment. Now has come a period of reflection and rethinking out of life's priorities and a sense of guilt at not being involved in the student activities that characterized the 60s.

Some of the stresses on today's students come from factors that are inherent in an academic situation. Procrastination is rampant on campuses. The closer attention of high-school teachers and the scrutiny of parents gives way to a new freedom which a student all too easily misuses and may come to the conclusion of a course in a state of near panic. Separation from home and family or familiar circumstances, although long sought, when it arrives often leaves the student with a sense of detachment and nonrelatedness. Competition from peers mounts in social activities and moves to an academic climax in examinations that build up stress in the academic pressure cooker. And in what might seem to be the most ironic situation of all, one of the most potent stressors will be in making a career choice. After all the years of study the graduate may discover he lacks the basic background for the work to which he should put his hand for a lifetime.

Later years may be characterized by a constant looking back to these college days, but despite this later attitude of "those were the days," at the time they were being lived they were frequently days of stress.

Choosing a mate is itself a test that will leave any multiple choice exams standing still. Vividly aware of a demanding libido, lured on by the somewhat less than realistic expectations of romantic love, unconvinced by any logic that even suggests a waiting period, the frail barque is launched on the Sea of Matrimony. Even if the matrimonial venture is successful enough to survive those tempests that wreck nearly half the marriages, there are yet other stressors laying in wait.

The home has traditionally been seen as the "shock absorber of the society," a haven to which a person could retreat from the hostility and struggles of the competitive business world and regroup the physical and emotional forces to prepare oneself to return to face it all anew. Now the picture may be changing and instead of the "shock absorber" the family may itself become the "shock deliverer." These shocks come from a number of changes that have taken place within the family.

The commitment to trying to earn as much a share as possible of the affluent society may mean that both husband and wife face the necessity to work outside the home. This work will give the family a two-salary income which will enable them to keep up with the Joneses, but will also bring a series of strains on the family members. All things being equal this could have a negative effect on the stability of the family.

One of the more obvious points of tension is likely to be the division of labor within the home. The move of women towards working outside the home has meant a departure from the traditional role of the wife staying at home and caring for the affairs of the house to going out to help to earn the living. Rather unfortunately the husband who is happy to see the wife earn money by leaving her traditional role at home still expects her to fulfill the role of housekeeper and is not happy to hear the news from her that she expects him to help her with the housework.

If a husband takes the nontraditional view that the wife should go out to work and combines with it a traditional view that she should be mainly responsible for the household chores, it may create an intolerable situation for the wife. It has been estimated the woman in full-time employment with sole responsibility of running the house can end up working as many as eighty hours a week. The tension can easily rise to intolerable levels.

The higher the commitment of both the husband and wife to work as a fulfilling experience the more likely it is the tensions will arise. Basically it comes down to whose job comes first, how much time will be spent with the family, and, ultimately, should there even be a family.

Then there is the much-vaunted standard of living in our free American society with its cornucopia of good things flowing from our industry and technology to our citizenry. When American flyers were captured by North Vietnamese,[4] we worried about what might happen to them, and when they returned we waited to see the effects of the years of incarceration upon them. It was true that many of them had dental problems and difficulty with parasitic infections, but, for a nation concerned about cardiovascular problems, the state of their health caused some raised eyebrows. Living under extremely difficult circumstances, the five years on a limited diet, reduced smoking, no alcohol, and their self-disciplined exercise programs had kept these men remarkably healthy. Compared with a matched group of flyers who had never been captured, the results showed that the nonprisoners had four times as much heart disease and high blood pressure than did the prisoners.

The situation is further complicated by the proposal set forth in this book that Christian resources should be used in the struggle with stress. Leading out in providing this help should be the minister of the gospel who should come ready to apply the balm of Gilead to the troubled soul. Rather unfortunately, the ministry is one of the most stressful of all occupations and many of our ministers who preach a gospel of serenity and security are themselves sometimes less than advertisements for the very gospel they preach.

It starts early when the college student announces he is a "ministerial student." He is immediately expected to be different and his life to reflect some piety notably absent from his fellow students. While others around him are sowing their "wild oats," he tries to look as if he is finding another source of enjoyment in life. Once in the seminary, where he has gone to take his training to prepare him for his work, he discovers a somewhat esoteric world in which otherworldly talk is the order of the day and where there are men and women who have come with a variety of motivations. In the midst of all this the would-be minister moves in an atmosphere that is somewhat different from the "peace, perfect peace" and "still waters" portrayed in the Bible he studies.

Graduation from seminary brings its own particular stresses as the new minister searches for a suitable position. Having spent at least seven years in college and seminary, he rightly expects at least a fair living but discovers church life to be a bittersweet experience. He is leading a democratic organization in which many people feel they have the right to tell him what they expect from him and make him wonder about his status. Although he inwardly compares himself to the other professionals in the community, the attorney, the doctor, the accountant, when he looks at his salary check he discovers it is often less than adequate.

This is the man who should be the greatest help to people who are stressed. He has the resources, the Christian traditions, concepts of prayer and meditation, the Bible with its age-old message. The problem is that this man or woman, who should be a primary source, is in a prime stressor occupation, and, consequently, finds it difficult to enthusiastically recommend the faith he represents to a person who is stressed.

However, these events that are so stressful may give the minister a background of personal experience that will enable him to be more understanding with people who come to him with stress-related difficulties. And he has some distinctive spiritual resources which he may demonstrate by his own ability to cope and which he will willingly share with a troubled parishioner.

2
The Gauguin Fantasy

Paul Gauguin (pronounced Gōgan), the famous French painter, was born in Paris in 1848. He not only influenced modern art but also lived one of the strangest and most colorful lives of any nineteenth-century artist. As a boy his parents took him to Peru where they lived for several years. Following his return to France as a young man, he enlisted in the Merchant Marine and sailed on the France and South American route. Then, apparently having satisfied his youthful wanderlust, he returned to Paris to settle down as part of bourgeois Parisian life.

In the year 1871, Paul Gauguin entered the world of business and obtained a position with the House of Bertin where he worked as a stockbroker. After two years of work, Gauguin was so successful that he felt confident enough to launch upon the sea of matrimony. He proposed to, and was accepted by, Mette Gad, a young Danish girl. The years following his marriage were the high point of his career in the world of commerce, during which he produced a very respectable income. During Paul Gauguin's twelve-year stretch in business, he gave every indication of being highly successful as an operator in that heart of French business life, the stock exchange. His success in business was matched by his domestic development as he fathered a family of five children.

As befitted a Parisian businessman, Paul Gauguin had a

hobby—he turned to the paint brush and palette and became what was often referred to as a "Sunday painter." His interest in painting grew until he decided to resign his stockbroker position to give his total energies to his artistic endeavors. Apparently his wife was unaware of this decision until after the event.

Gauguin's rather cavalier attitude towards earning a living antagonized his wife's family, and he, in turn, increasingly perceived them as working against him. In the year 1887, he crossed his Rubicon when he made his great decision and announced to his wife that he had decided to move to the island of Martinique where he intended to "live as a savage."

Later, in pursuit of his aim to "live as a savage," in his forty-third year, Gauguin went to Tahiti where he turned aside from the European community which represented a style of life he'd grown to despise, and went to live among the natives. From among these natives he took a common-law wife who bore him a son as he continued his quest for a life close to nature. On one occasion he wrote with a sense of self-satisfaction, "My life is now that of a savage."

At fifty-five years of age, now living in the Marquesas Islands, having attempted suicide three years earlier, suffering from syphilis and the aftermath of a stroke, Gauguin died surrounded by lush tropical flora, but bereft of human companionship. It is not without significance that his last painting executed in the exotic tropics, was not of voluptuous island beauties, but of a snow scene in his native France.

The Gauguin fantasy has continued to haunt the minds of many people. Wearying of the humdrum of everyday working responsibilities there comes the haunting fantasy of a place where the lotus eaters live. Here may be found the noble savage, sensuous living, carefree days in the sun. It sometimes starts in early days with children dreaming dreams and lured on by their Pied Piper; the tumultuous days of adolescence in the struggle between sensuality, idealism, and a desire to be loved, looking for a heaven, not on a tropical island but in a big city, that all too easily turns into a hellish nightmare. In adulthood it may be the poor man's divorce, as a husband tiring of his responsibilities slips away from home; and, more recently, the runaway wife, in violation of traditional mother love lore, disappears overnight. It manifests itself in many different forms, but a good proportion of society's dropouts are victims of the Gauguin fantasy.

Martin Luther stood at exactly the opposite end of the continuum from Gauguin. Until Luther's day, the official church position was that work was punishment for sin. When Adam sinned, part of the penalty was that he should work. "Not so," said Luther. He saw a man's work as his calling from God. Before Luther the word *vocation* referred to a calling to a life in a monastery where the subject spent his life worshiping God. Luther proudly proclaimed that the man who shoveled the manure and the woman who milked the cow might be doing a work more pleasing to God than the monk in the monastery who spent his day praying and singing psalms. Two centuries later John Wesley took up the same idea of the value of work and urged his followers to "earn all you can."

The man who had a viable religious experience saw his work as the calling of God and worked more industriously earning more money. At the same time he also became more frugal, no longer spending his money on worldly pleasures. So has come:

Spend Less + Earn More = Accumulation

Some authorities believe this may have been an important consideration in the development of capitalism.

While conducting a conference in a large city, I noticed a number of poorly dressed men sitting around the parking lot of an elegant church building. They sat, smoked, and looked off into space, some periodically taking a surreptitious mouthful from a bottle. It turned out these men were waiting for the opening of a mission a couple of blocks down the street where they could get a free meal. These "winos," as they are sometimes called, are a strange nomadic group who represent an attitude towards life of "why bother?" They live their days from handout to handout with little concern for what a day may bring forth. Many of these men are victims of the Gauguin fantasy.

The church, in the parking lot of which the "winos" sat around awaiting their handout, a hive of activity with its membership of dedicated businessmen and their families represented a group of people committed to the Luther ethic. Industrious and ambitious, their religious commitment encouraged them to see their work as a vocation—a calling from God. If by some chance they were separated from their work, they would be frustrated and unhappy.

Figure 1. The tension of modern man is between living an industrious, competitive, responsible life in the Luther tradition and the carefree life of the indolent in the Gauguin life-style.

It seems unfair that the businessmen whose efforts made it possible for the society to support the "winos" might be prime candidates for the illnesses associated with the stresses of business life. Unlike the "winos" who had walked out on their family responsibilities, these church people were altogether wrapped up in the events of their family lives, which in turn brought other stressors to bear upon them.

In a way it may be the ultimate contradiction, in a society like the United States which exemplifies just what may be accomplished by adherence to the Luther ethic, the follower of this ethic will one day come to a time when he will be required to leave his work which he has been taught across the years to see as the calling of God. His experience is described under the euphemism of "retirement," with the implication that the businessman, worn out with his years of work, is at last given a reprieve from his sentence and able to rest from his labors. Because Bismarck, the Prussian leader in the nineteenth century noted that life expectancy was about forty years, he arbitrarily decided sixty-five, an age which only a minority reached, would represent the ultimate in years for a human, and so decreed this as the retirement age. Most Western societies fell into line and in a day when the average life expectancy in the United States has come to be seventy plus years it is only with great difficulty that the age of retirement has been recently partially raised to seventy.

Retirement is a rationalization which is portrayed as a reward for hard work but in reality becomes one of modern man's most traumatic stresses. If an individual is careless about his work, irresponsible in his attitudes to his employer, casual in his loyalties, a "goof-off," retirement will indeed be a virtual paradise, a fervently longed-for goal that will bring delightful years of idleness.

If, on the other hand, the individual conscientiously hones his skills, painstakingly disciplines himself, so that by his diligence he comes to find great enjoyment in his work, retirement will be one of the most traumatic events of his life. On the Holmes and Rohe Social Readjustment Scale of one to a hundred, measuring the effect traumatic events have on an individual, retirement measures forty-five. So comes one of the contradictions of our society. We reward loyalty and diligence with a punishment by taking away the very thing the practitioner of the Luther ethic values most of all—his work.

The stuff Gauguin's fantasy was made of is the human being's capacity to image. Man has been called an imaging being. This capacity is a peculiar human phenomenon, cats and dogs don't envisage a situation different from that in which they exist. Man's capacity for imaging has meant he has a mental process that has opened the whole group of peculiar possibilities. He can take the Gauguin route and be occupied with fantasies of tropical islands, native beauties, carefree living, and following this fantasy, he will walk out on his responsibilities and live in a strange, nonexistent, nowhere land.

But there is another side to the human capacity for visualization. In a recent magazine article, the author called for a greater use of daydreaming and points out that many of the great creative personalities have been people whom he calls "daydreamers." He points out that Thomas Edison stretched out on his workshop couch and let fantasies fill his mind. Claud Debussy established an atmosphere of creativity while gazing at the golden reflections of the setting sun in the river Seine. Schiller kept a rotting apple in his desk drawer and the aroma evoked a mood of reverie. Dostoevski doodled as he dreamed up his moving stories and characters. The author adds, "Daydreaming may promote emotional health."[1]

But there is all the world of difference between the daydream or fantasy and the vision. Both use imaging, but the visionary has a picture on the screen of his mind of something hitherto unknown which can be accomplished. A major distinction between the fantasy and the vision is that the vision will call for hard work, dedication, and commitment but it may ultimately become a reality. By way of contrast, the fantasy is an indication of an easy way out, and, for the indolent, an escape from life.

This distinction would be seen in an oil exploration team working in the desert. They are looking for something they cannot directly see, a pool of oil far below the earth's surface. They make seismographic soundings, picturing in their minds what the formations of layers of the earth below might be and whether they would really contain the oil they need so badly.

As the exploration team works in the burning heat one of the men points to a beautiful scene in the distance. There is a green oasis, fountains of sparkling water, date palms, fruit trees, green lawns, shelter, water, food, ease. The major problem is that it has no reality. The mirage will lure them on, but retreat as quickly as they chase it.

The difference between the two, the vision and the fantasy is to be seen in what it does to the beholder. The fantasy, completely unreal, leading nowhere, providing an escape from responsibility; the vision calling for energy and hard work commitment; the fantasy bringing surcease to the individual; the vision bringing a sense of struggle and achievement with effects that spread to the lives of others.

Now has come another aspect to the imaging process. To the vision and the fantasy must be added the process we call reverie. It is part of the total meditation experience. Here is an aspect of human experience awaiting to be developed.

In our discussion we will explore some of the neglected possibilities in the factor which separates man from animal—the imaging process. The businessman who turns aside from the Gauguin fantasy to live his life by the Luther ethic can have the best of two worlds. Not only does he have the satisfaction of meaningful work, bringing its peculiar joy as an act of creativity, but also he can learn to use his imaging capacity to cope with the stress which his work commitment brings. Reports have come of businesses where the employees, instead of stimulating themselves with coffee in the morning break, are taking a relaxation break. In this experience they will utilize imaging, creating pictures in their minds, but these pictures and thoughts will help them to cope with life and be creative producers.

3
An Age-Old Safeguard Becomes a Modern Scourge

Beekeeping has been called the "gentle art," and that designation gives the beekeeper the clue to the way needed to handle bees—gently. No bumps, noises, or quick movements.

When I was first introduced to a bee colony, I knew from my reading exactly the way I should approach the situation. I was to show no fear, remain cool, calm, and collected, move easily into the situation and there was little danger that I would ever be stung. I had learned to look at the experience from a beekeeper's perspective which is that bees never attack people. Bees only defend themselves from what they interpret as an offensive against them. When it is all said and done, if a bee stings a human it is the end of her life, she has nothing to gain from it. Bees only sting to defend, and incidentally, not themselves but the colony of bees.

Armed with this knowledge I approached the hive. A few curious bees flew in my direction to scout the newcomer. Though I knew intellectually there was nothing to fear, a strange apprehension began to mount within me. A couple of bees zoomed in close to my face. My heartbeat rate increased noticeably. Almost instinctively my hand disobeyed my intellect and flew up to bat off the visitors. Accidentally, I mashed two of the little honey gatherers and one of them replied by plunging her stinger into my finger. The rapid movement of my arm, the mashing of the bees, the aroma of the squashed body brought a wave of response as the other members of the colony came swarming around like a squadron of fighter planes and I turned and fled.

We were both, the bees and I, victims and demonstrators of an age-old mechanism that has served man and animal well in bygone days but in modern times has become a scourge to twentieth-century man.

It has long been recognized that the secret of the survival of some forms of animal life has lain in their use of two mechanisms developed in the infancy of the race and referred to as fight or flight. Faced with a life-threatening situation, the animal could launch a ferocious counterattack and frighten off the intruder. However, many animals were much weaker than their opponents and the only practical way out was to turn and run and hope to escape by their speed. In the realm of nature the attack or flee mechanism has been the secret of survival for many forms of animal life.

Nor is this confined to animals. Observers have long noted that humans have a similar reaction which was probably of first-rate importance for survival in the infancy of the race. Primitive man lived in a hostile environment of constant threat. At any moment a belligerent native, or a saber-toothed tiger, or some other enemy might spring upon him. Humans developed a mechanism similar to that of the animals that would help them to cope with these life-threatening situations.

In this type of reaction the whole body moved into an emergency mode in which the heart raced, breathing rate increased, blood pressure heightened, blood flowed to the muscles to ready them for action, and the rate of metabolism changed. All of these changes were preparing primitive man for either launching an attack upon, or racing away from the enemy. The reaction was either *active* through fight or *passive* by running away from it in flight.

The "fight or flight" reaction was valuable for primitive man, and frequently the secret of his survival. Unfortunately, the effectiveness and constant use of the fight or flight mechanism by primitive man has, in part, led to modern man's undoing and downfall. In modern society neither fighting nor fleeing are appropriate for most of the situations we face. The result is that while modern man's body is periodically geared up for the two actions of fighting and running, neither is desirable in modern twentieth-century living.

Of course, the threats modern man faces are of a different kind. Few of us will ever encounter a tiger. Our threat is more likely to be a letter from the Internal Revenue Service about an impending audit, a confronting interview with the boss, filing of divorce papers, or a note from the school principal about the children's behavior. Each of these situations may ring alarm bells within us but in none of these is the fight or flight reaction appropriate.

To further complicate the situation we live in a society which encourages aggressive attitudes, but in theory at least, eschews violence. The dilemma is nowhere more clearly dramatized then in the great American pastime of football. A football game has been described as twenty-two men on the field in need of a rest and 65,000 people in the stands in desperate need of exercise. The men on the field need a rest because they are in a struggle in which aggression is highly prized. One of the often repeated objectives is the Vince Lombardi statement, "Winning is not the main thing—it's the only thing."

The man who became to college football what Lombardi

was to the professional game was Woody Hayes of Ohio State. Hayes took up the same theme, "This country is built on winning and on that alone." He established a reputation with a team he fired to the heights of enthusiasm. On one occasion, at least, his intensity created a problem. Nervously moving along the sidelines during the 1978 Gator Bowl in the encounter between Ohio State and Clemson University, Hayes was horrified to see the middle guard of opposing Clemson intercept an Ohio State pass. As the interceptor came racing down the sideline, Hayes impulsively stepped up and delivered a roundhouse punch to the player's head.

The coach's action typifies the dilemma of modern man. He must be aggressive to achieve and, if he is a leader, motivate the aggressive impulses of his followers. But through it all, our society insists that he remain calm and unperturbed. The Gator Bowl incident cost Woody Hayes his job and left him a sad and frustrated man.

With the supreme confidence so characteristic of modern man, we frequently get the idea that all the problems of life can be easily handled, overlooking the tenacity of primitive forces. Possibly no single person did more to dramatize the possibilities of a relationship between man and animal than did Joy Adamson. European-born Joy married a British-Irish game warden, and though childless, this couple established a "family" of foundling animals.

In 1956 Joy rescued a newly born cub from certain death. The cub, named Elsa, became a family pet who rode on the roof of their Land Rover and often slept in their tent. The saga of Elsa grew into one of the great human interest stories of the century and was immortalized in the movie, *Born Free.* Later Joy realized the lioness, along with other animals that had become a part of this extraordinary family, needed to be returned to the freedom of the forest. Much of Joy's time was given to a program of detraining the animals and returning them to their natural habitat.

The monument to her work, into which Joy Adamson plowed the profits of her books and movie, was an organization named the Elsa Wild Animal Appeal and symbolized the way humans could help animals. In January 1980, Joy took her usual evening stroll and failed to return. A search party found her dead body. She had either been mauled by a lion or attacked by a disaffected native. The primitive forces of nature personified by either native or beast had triumphed over the civilized European. In much the same way the fight or flight mechanism had continued to be a thorn in the side of modern man.

The way in which modern man comes to terms with his fight or flight mechanism and brings it under control will in large measure determine the quality of his life. In the ultimate irony a mechanism that developed originally for the purpose of preserving life has become the most significant factor in the destruction of the delicate body machinery. What had evolved to save humans from the enemy without has itself become the enemy within.

4
Stress and Distress

The search for the cause of heart disease was notably advanced by two unlikely people—an upholsterer (male) and the president (female) of a Junior League. Each made observations—one inadvertently and the other intentionally—and helped to establish an idea.

A prominent medical researcher remembers these two people clearly. He and his fellow investigator had long been convinced about diet, smoking, and lack of exercise as factors in heart attacks, but an upholsterer working in the reception room of the two doctors' office unwittingly raised another issue when he asked the doctor what type of practice he engaged in. In being told the partners were cardiologists, the doctor asked the upholsterer why he wanted to know. His reply, "It's so peculiar that only the front edge of your chairs are worn out." To the chair expert it was clear the patients of these doctors were under a special constraint.

Later the same doctor talked with the president of the Junior League as they discussed the importance of diet and heart disease. An effort was being made to compare the diet of women, who had few heart attacks, and their husbands, who were much more prone to heart disease. This woman verbalized her doubts that diet was the problem then went on to present her own nonmedical hypothesis, "It's stress, the stress they receive in their work, that's doing it."[1]

These and other experiences led the two cardiologists to

postulate that it might not be so much the physical factors of diet, condition of blood vessels, the circumstances of life, or lack of exercise, but rather the distinctive personality of the individual, that a certain type of personality—what they call Type A— might be the all-important consideration in people who fell victim to a heart attack.

This hypothesis was the more remarkable because these two medical doctors were men who had spent their days studying the human body, how it worked, and what caused it to malfunction. They were talking about personality, the mental processes, attitudes, the realm of the psychologist. They finally came up with their ideas about two personality types—Type A and Type B.

They described the types as:

The Behavior Pattern of a Type A Person

1. A habit of explosively accentuating various key words and a tendency to utter the last few words of a sentence more rapidly than the opening
2. Always moving, walking, and eating rapidly
3. A feeling of impatience with the rate at which events are taking place
4. Striving to think or do two or more things simultaneously
5. Experiencing difficulty in refraining from talking or walking or bringing the theme of the conversation around to those subjects of special interest to the subject
6. A vaguely guilty feeling when relaxing or doing absolutely nothing for several hours to several days
7. No longer observing the important, interesting, or lovely things in the environment
8. No time to spare on things worth *being* because preoccupied with things worth *having*

9. A tendency to schedule more and more things in less and less time and developing a sense of chronic time urgency
10. When coming into contact with another Type A personality, there is a drive to confront that personality
11. Resorting to certain characteristic gestures or nervous tics such as clenching the fist or jaw or grinding the teeth
12. A belief that success has come because of an ability to get things done faster than others
13. Constantly translating and evaluating one's own and others' activities in terms of numbers

If an employer were looking for an employee to head up some new program, this is probably the type of person he would seek. A driving, aggressive businessman who could really "cut the mustard" is much sought after in the business world. Should the Type A hypothesis be correct, it may be that our society is sending our businessmen, and more recently our businesswomen, on dangerous and hazardous missions. They are not unlike the kamikaze pilots of World War II who were sent out with the order to gain a victory but to do it with the certainty that a successful mission meant that the combatant had to sacrifice his own life. The businessman becomes the kamikaze pilot of today, working hard to make sure that his wife and family are well cared for and provided with the material wherewithal whereby they can survive in this world. To accomplish this he has to be willing to sacrifice himself and leave the family devoid of his presence. It may be that the price is too much to pay.

In contrast to the Type A personality, Friedman and Rosenman have come up with what they call Type B behavior pattern. A person is said to be a Type B when he exhibits the following characteristics:

Type B Behavior Pattern

1. If you are completely free of *all* the habits and exhibit none of the traits we have listed that harass the severely afflicted Type A person
2. If you never suffer from a sense of time urgency with its accompanying impatience
3. If you harbor no free-floating hostility, and you feel no need to display or discuss either your achievements or accomplishments unless such exposure is demanded by the situation
4. If, when you play, you do so to find fun and relaxation, not to exhibit your superiority at any cost
5. If you can relax without guilt, just as you can work without agitation.[2]

The concept of Type A and Type B personalities has been very influential, but it is not without its critics. One of the most obvious areas for criticism is the Type B which seems to indicate that the most important thing in life is to sit down, fold your hands, and do nothing. While visiting an internist for my annual checkup, I mentioned my interest in exercise and looked for an affirming response. The internist smiled, made a condescending remark about the doctors who wrote books concerning the importance of exercise, and smirked that they had probably made "a bunch of money," then went on to make a point about the strain exercise programs imposed on the patients. His point was that spending so much time and striving so hard to earn aerobic points were indicative of Type A behavior and might be actually doing more damage to the heart.

Stunned by his antiexercise attitude, I looked at him a little closer, noted his "paunch," and suddenly realized that I, his patient, was being counseled in terms of his personal life-style which apparently had little place for exercise. As we will shortly notice, Dr. Glasser has seen the great value of "Positive Addiction" which calls for a vigorous commitment to some type of activity. Preeminent among the activities which Glasser recommends is a program that includes two prime activities—jogging and meditation, and Dr. Selye "the Father of Stress" whom we will now consider, has a large place in his program for activity.

The man whose name is most closely associated with the stress concept is Dr. Hans Selye who, following his medical education in Europe, migrated to America, settled in Canada, and developed a theory of stress. At seventy-one years of age Dr. Selye founded the International Institute of Stress on the campus of the University of Montreal and works twelve-hour days on problems associated with stress.

Selye began his research with animals and was impressed with the General Adaptations Syndrome [G.A.S.] which went through three stages—(1) the alarm reaction; (2) the stage of resistance; and (3) the stage of exhaustion. He came to see these three stages as analogous to three stages of man's life: "childhood (with its characteristic low resistance and excessive responses to any kind of stimulus), adulthood (during which adaptation to most commonly encountered agents has occurred and resistance is increased), and finally, senility (characterized by irreversible loss of adaptability and eventual exhaustion) ending with death."[3]

We might note that Selye at seventy-one years of age gives few indications of losing his capacity to adapt. In an interview he told about the problems fame had brought, as people in public places such as the airport, seeking either to visit, or to get a free consultation, were constantly harassing him. He resorted to wearing a wig or dark glasses but found them ineffective, so he looked to nature where he noticed a little black animal that seemed to have effectively solved the problem of unwanted company. He describes the way he applied the principle of nature, "I now travel with a few bulbs of garlic in my pocket and when cornered chew them like gum. I happen to like the taste, but sooner or later the other person always mumbles something and departs—leaving me happily to my privacy."[4]

Selye says, "Adaptability is probably the most distinctive characteristic of life." I would like to state the situation even more strongly, *The secret of human survival is man's capacity for adaptation.* When a human fails to adapt, he falls into a condition we call stress. One man described his internal reaction in certain of the situations which he constantly faced, "I feel as if I have lost control, life gets out of hand, other people are making decisions that affect me and I cannot do anything about it." It is not easy to adapt to such a situation as this and it leads to stress.

Those of us who lived through World War II can remember some of the drastic changes that can take place in a time of national emergency. The normal political processes may be temporarily suspended, movement restricted, the economy managed in ways intolerable in normal times, goods and services rationed, peace-loving citizens conscripted to the task of killing their fellow humans, people deprived of many of their civil liberties, the media censored. Most of these actions would be completely unacceptable in normal times but in the face of a threat to national existence they are seen not only as acceptable but necessary.

A similar situation may come to pass in a time of stress. In reaction to what is perceived as a threat, the whole body moves into a series of new emergency functions, hearing becomes more sensitive, the vision clearer, the stomach slows down its digestive process, the heart races, the breath may come in a more rapid manner. As Albrecht says it, "The stress reaction is a coordinated chemical mobilization of the entire human body to meet the requirements of life and death struggles or of rapid escape from the situation."[5]

The tragedy of all this is that it is possible to win a war and finish up a loser. Look at World War II in which Japan and Germany were both defeated and surrendered, yet in the years following the war emerged economically stronger than some of the so-called victors in the conflict. As Albrecht says: "The human body—your body—is capable of literally destroying itself when it is forced to maintain a high-stress alarm state for long periods without relief."[6] The situation is reminiscent of the classical story of Pyrrhus who, as he walked through the battlefield in which he had won the battle, looked over the bodies of the fallen, the scattered and destroyed equipment, and lamented, "Another victory like this and I shall be ruined." The subject of stress, no matter what personal satisfaction it has gained, has really won a Pyrrhic victory.

Twentieth-century mobility is another factor in the stress situation. Modern life has become so much more a matter of movement than it was for primitive man who grew, lived, and died in one small locale. By way of contrast, twentieth-century Americans are constantly on the move. The one unchanging fact for modern man is that everything will change. These changes aggravate the problems of coping with life as is seen in the Holmes and Rohe study of 394 individuals.

From an examination of the experiences of these people the researchers came up with a Social Readjustment Scale. This scale is seen in figure 1.

Again comes the recurring paradox. Some of the stresses that cause so much trouble are positive and are what would normally be called joyous events. It might well be imagined these events would be stress relievers rather than stressors.

The situation is pointed up by the humorous story of a father-son interaction. After reading about the dangers of forty-year plus men shoveling wet snow, the father sat down with his eldest son. The father carefully explained that men over forty years of age who shoveled wet snow often put themselves in potential danger of a heart attack.

FATHER: "Because of this possibility that the labor of shoveling wet snow might bring on a heart attack, I am wondering if you would shovel the snow for me?"

SON: "Sure, Pop. I'll go out right away and do it."

The father clasped his hands to his chest, collapsed, and fell to the floor in the agony of a heart attack.

In the list of stresses are such events as marital reconciliation, gaining a new family member, outstanding personal achievement, vacational periods, and Christmas. Though normally considered to be happy occasions they, nevertheless, became stresses in some people's lives.

A second paradox in the findings of the Holmes Study was that 50 percent of the 300 plus people did *not* get sick during the period under examination, pointing up the importance of the individual's temperament. Earlier we referred to the incident in which the volatile college football coach, Woody Hayes, punched a player on the opposing team. Contrast Hayes with the professional football coach, Tom Landry of the Dallas Cowboys. Landry has an entirely different tem-

THE STRESS OF ADJUSTING TO CHANGE[7]

Events	Scale of Impact
Death of spouse	100
Divorce	73
Marital separation	65
Jail term	63
Death of close family member	63
Personal injury or illness	53
Marriage	50
Fired at work	47
Marital reconciliation	45
Retirement	45
Change in health of family member	44
Pregnancy	40
Sex difficulties	39
Gain of new family member	39
Business readjustment	39
Change in financial state	38
Death of close friend	37
Change to different line of work	36
Change in number of arguments with spouse	35
Mortgage over $10,000	31
Foreclosure of mortgage or loan	30
Change in responsibilities at work	29
Son or daughter leaving home	29
Trouble with in-laws	29
Outstanding personal achievement	28
Wife begins or stops work	26
Begin or end school	26
Change in living conditions	25
Revision of personal habits	24
Trouble with boss	23
Change in work hours or conditions	20
Change in residence	20
Change in schools	20
Change in recreation	19
Change in church activities	19
Change in social activities	18
Mortgage or loan less than $10,000	17
Change in sleeping habits	16
Change in number of family get-togethers	15
Change in eating habits	15
Vacation	13
Christmas	12
Minor violations of the law	11

Figure 1

perament than the excitable Hayes. Always impeccably dressed with a fedora tipped at just the right angle, in the heat and stress of the game, Landry is recently said by one writer to have a face which knows two expressions—disinterested, and "Where am I?" Game plan sheet in hand, he gazes down at the complicated plays as if exploring the possibilities of an itinerary for his next summer's vacation. The personality of the patient has long been recognized in all forms of medicine. Speaking of physical illness a medical doctor once said, "It is sometimes more important to know what kind of a fellow has the germ than what kind of germ has the fellow." The stress situation is even more closely interrelated with the personality of the subject.

Situation factors enter to complicate the picture. John B. Watson, referred to in a recent biography as "the father of behaviorism" had a spectacular career in the field of psychology. At twenty-nine years of age he occupied the chair in psychology at Johns Hopkins University and was elected president of the American Psychological Association at age thirty-six. Then things went wrong, and Watson was a party to what was referred to in that day as a "scandalous divorce." Unable to gain another university appointment, and ignored by his colleagues in psychology, Watson sought a position in advertising where he went on to a successful career.

Although Watson achieved considerable wealth, the following thirty-five years were spent apart from the world of psychology. An article in a psychological journal in 1956, written by Gustav Bergman, claimed Watson's contribution to psychology was second only to Freud's and in an incidental way the writer mentioned that Watson at seventy-seven years of age was still alive. The news struck a responsive chord among psychologists and in 1957 the American Psychological Association decided to confer a gold medal upon Watson and in the citation referred to him as "one of the vital determinants of the form and substance of modern psychology."

Watson was apparently delighted with the news of the honor and accepted an invitation to come to the American Psychological Association meeting in New York for the presentation of the medal. With his two sons and his secretary he stayed in a nearby hotel. But on the day of the presentation Watson could not bring himself to go to the meeting and made an agonizing decision not to personally accept the coveted award. He sent his son Billy to take his place. For Watson the situation of accepting a long-desired honor under these circumstances was too much for him to handle. An apparent triumph and vindication became a stressor.

The Varieties of Stress

From what we have said it might be imagined the ideal way to live would be to seek some secluded spot to which to retreat. In this sheltered place life could be lived without any intrusions that might in any way bring about the state referred to as stress.

According to Dr. Selye this is not so. He sees stress as an experience that comes in different shapes and sizes. He particularly specifies three conditions hypostress, stress, and eustress.

Hypostress is the term Selye uses to describe a condition in

HYPOSTRESS   EUSTRESS   STRESS

which there is too little stress in an individual's life. There is little external stimuli and an absence of activity. This consideration has led Selye to speculate about the value of techniques which call for the subject to spend his days in meditation. Psychiatrist Beach agrees with Selye and says, "There is no such thing as living totally free of stress. Just staying alive creates stress. Those under no stress are in the graveyard. Even when people retire, stress doesn't stop. They are free from work stress, but they are also free from human contact, and that in itself creates a great deal of stress."[8] So, complete absence of stress is not a true objective in life.

In a recent interview Dr. Selye (Dr. Stress to his fellow citizens in Montreal, Canada), in response to a question as to how he coped with stress said, "By being as busy with my work as I possibly can. I almost always put in at least a ten-hour day, and often more. This week, for example, along with receiving visitors to our new International Institute of Stress here in Montreal, attending staff conferences, and writing various papers, I'll be making speeches in cities both inside and outside Canada. And far from being wearied by this typically hectic schedule, I find that I positively flourish on it."[9] Would Friedman say he was a Type A personality?

Dr. Selye emphasizes the importance of the stressors that are the cause of a stressed person's condition. He makes a comparison of two people under stress, a man in a dentist chair, and one who is exchanging a passionate kiss with his lover. Their reactions may be the same, racing pulse, quickened breathing, soaring heartbeat, yet who would deliberately avoid the second or seek the first experience?

Selye divides people into two categories: "racehorses" who thrive on stress and need a fast vigorous life, and "turtles" who must have a tranquil environment. Selye admits he falls into the "racehorse" category and says, "I could hardly imagine any torture worse than having to lie on a beach doing nothing day after day, yet, in my travels, I've noticed a great many people whose chief aim in life is to be able to do precisely that."[10]

Selye has many knowledgeable people who would willingly back him up on this position. One of these is Dr. Glasser. Glasser postulates an experience which he calls Positive Addiction. The criteria he sets down for Positive Addiction are:

1. It is something noncompetitive that you choose to do and you can devote an hour (approximately) a day to it.
2. It is possible for you to do it easily and it doesn't take a great deal of mental effort to do it well.
3. You can do it alone or rarely with others but it does not depend upon others to do it.
4. You believe that it has some value (physical, mental, or spiritual) for you.
5. You believe that if you persist at it you will improve, but this is completely subjective—you need to be the only one who measures that improvement.
6. The activity must have the quality that you can do it without criticizing yourself. If you can't accept yourself during this time, the activity will not be addicting.[11]

This last element may be the all-important consideration. If you are comfortable in your activity, don't worry about what other people think about it, it will pay its dividends to you.

On Sunday, September 23, 1979, the Fort Worth, Texas Convention Center was the scene of a "tractor pull." In this event a modified tractor, the hot-rod of the tractor world, was attempting to pull a thirty-five-ton sled along a 200-foot track. Straining to move the load, the powerful machine gave off a barrage of earsplitting sounds that half-deafened the huge crowd. The sound level suddenly moved to a new high and the tractor transmission exploded into a hail of flying metal which injured at least fifteen of the people watching the event.

The tractor transmission might well represent the dilemma of modern man. On the one hand, like the high-powered engine, the compelling primitive forces of personality push for urgent action. On the other hand, the requirements of modern living, like that thirty-five-ton sled, continue to hold us in place. The pressures mount, the demands of society grow, and our personalities, like the transmission, capitulate to the intolerable strain.

But there is another consideration that enters to complicate the situation. This "tractor pull," presented as an entertainment, represented a gross misuse of the tractor's power. The machine was designed for farm operations. In this role the tractor has made possible an agriculture that has produced food not only for the United States but a good proportion of the world and has made American agriculture the wonder of our age. Used for entertainment rather than cultivation, the tractor suddenly became destructive rather than creative. People, like tractors, have tremendous powers within their bodies which they can all too easily misuse and turn themselves into "hot rods" and explode under the pressures, or they can take the same forces and channel them into productive and creative ends.

5
A Silent Killer
Has an Accomplice

Groups of doctors in different parts of the country participated in a unique continuing education program, utilizing television hook-ups to bring physicians living in twenty-six cities in contact with each other. Stress was the subject under discussion and it was stated at the outset that "it appears that stress could be implicated in about 20 to 50 percent of all patient visits in the United States each year. That's almost as frequent as the common cold."[1] Then the study document made an important distinction, "There is a difference between stress and the common cold, however. The common cold is a disease. *Stress is not a disease.*"

If stress is not a disease, why were all these medical doctors studying this entity? They were engaged in this study because the effects of stress are pervasive and can trigger many symptoms. Almost all the ills that attack the human body are exacerbated by stress. Because stress is a factor that is not obvious, one way to view its effects would be to concentrate on one malfunction of the human body and see how it is affected. For this purpose we will focus on what is referred to as "The Silent Killer" and has become a problem of such magnitude that a war has been declared on hypertension or high blood pressure. In this chapter we will examine high blood pressure as an example of just one condition very much affected by stress.

An America faced with ever-diminishing energy resources

has been compelled not only to think of new resources but also of the pipeline used to transport this precious commodity from wellhead to point of consumption. The Alaska pipeline, stretching from Prudhoe Bay to the port of Valdez, with all its special provisions to prevent the damage of the sensitive environment and keep the precious fuel moving through it, is one of the wonders of modern technology. As wonderful as is this pipeline system, it is dwarfed into insignificance when we look into the cardiovascular system within the complex human body.

Just imagine a pipeline stretching from New York to San Francisco to Houston to Miami and back up the East Coast to New York again and see it running around the perimeter of the country five times over. You now have something of a picture of the combined length of the labyrinth of blood vessels, about 62,000 miles, in the human body. At the center of this is a pumping station which keeps the blood moving through the pipes. This pumping station which we call the heart is the most important muscle of the body and pumps at the rate of seventy times a minute which amounts to 100,000 times a day, climbing to a half-billion times in seventy years. This amounts to about forty-six billion gallons of blood which is pumped through the pipeline in our lifetime.

One writer has estimated that the force needed to pump this much liquid, if it were possible to harness it in a single instant, would lift a ten-ton weight ten miles into the air. This pressure pushes the blood away from the heart against the artery walls, not as a steady, unrelenting pressure, but one which changes from moment to moment, reaching its peak each time that the heart beats, decreasing to a minimum just before the next beat. The measure of an individual's blood is stated in two numbers—*systolic pressure*, the maximum when the heart beats, over the *diastolic pressure,* which is the minimum between beats. The pressure is measured in millimeters of mercury with the normal blood pressure reading being about 120/80.

A British clergyman named Steven Hales devised the first method of measuring blood pressure in the eighteenth century, using a funnel-like device to measure the blood pressure of a mare. Modern physicians usually use a sphygmomanometer, which has an inflatable cuff with a pressure gauge attached. The physician inflates the cuff around your upper arm until the blood stops circulating, then, pressing his stethoscope against an artery, listens as he reduces the pressure of the cuff. When he hears the sound of the blood spurting through, he notes the pressure display on the meter or column of mercury and has the systolic pressure. He continues to listen until the sound indicates the flow of blood is no longer interfered with and he has the diastolic pressure.

One of the problems in taking blood pressure is that it can change from moment to moment but some standards are fairly widely accepted. Blood pressure higher than 160/95 is generally referred to as *definite hypertension,* while the blood pressure between 140/90 and 160/95 is labeled *borderline hypertension.* A fairly normal figure would be somewhere around 120/80.

High blood pressure has been called the silent killer because it produces no pain and generally no other symptoms or warnings before wreaking havoc with the cardiovascular system and other organs. Hypertension is the primary cause of stroke and increases the risk of heart attacks and coronary artery disease and other cardiovascular problems which cause more Americans' deaths than all the other causes of death combined.

The insurance companies, sometimes referred to as "those great score keepers of American mortality," have developed charts that dispassionately predict just how many years you will live. In reading these conclusions it becomes clear that the primary factor in gauging mortality is blood pressure. Blood pressure has some strange effects on the human body and influences the heart, the kidneys, the brain, and the arteries.

During World War II, while serving as a chaplain with the Australian Army, I found myself with the responsibility for lecturing on venereal disease. In the process of my research I visited a psychiatric hospital where the medical officer showed me a number of patients in the final stages of syphilis (venereal disease). As I lamented the waste of life and declared my intention to strike a blow against this killer, the doctor quietly responded, "Why don't you use your abundant energies in a battle against what I consider to be a much greater danger to human beings—heart disease?"

I have now come to see the doctor's point and the center of this concern is that twelve-ounce, red-brown, six- by four-inch organ called the heart. One of its deadliest enemies is hypertension. When blood pressure is raised, the heart is compelled to work harder. If blood pressure is elevated 20 percent of normal the heart must work 20 percent harder. Like any other muscle which has to work more diligently, it increases in size. At first, it manages the load and then there comes a time when it cannot cope and congestive heart failure results. Hypertension causes damage to the heart as it leads to an enlarged heart which may result in congestive heart failure or coronary insufficiency or sometimes both.

When hypertension is longstanding it may affect the kidneys. As the blood supply to the kidneys is reduced they cease to function at full capacity and become less effective in ridding the body of waste products. Salt is retained and this fluid retention has deleterious effects on the heart.

That control center of the human body, called the brain, is an immensely complex three-pound mushroom of gray and white tissue of gelatinous consistency, containing some three billion neurons. The arteries which bring the life-giving blood to this intricate computer may have a blowout or a rupture. This brings on a condition known as a stroke, causing a part of the brain to starve. This result of high blood pressure may have effects ranging from mental lapses to total paralysis and to death.

Those complex pipelines that make up the circulatory system will naturally fall victim to the increased pressure upon them caused by hypertension. Strangely enough, it is a substance that becomes a part of the inside wall of the artery which is the villain. Atherosclerosis is a fatty streak on the inside of the artery containing an accumulation of cholesterol compounds, and some fats which continue to grow and ultimately obstruct the flow of blood through the artery. This blockage leads inexorably to a heart attack.

Evidence has been amassed to show that a number of factors go into the development of atherosclerosis—our modern diet, high in fat; obesity; cigarette smoking; sedentary living. Now has come the evidence for the not-so-obvious cause— hypertension. A series of studies have pointed to the following conclusions:

1. Hypertension intensifies any atherosclerosis that may stem from diet and the drug to control hypertension reverses this effect.
2. Hypertension increases the deposition of cholesterol on the artery wall and this increased deposition does

not depend upon increased blood cholesterol.
3. Hypertension increases the rate of cholesterol production in the liver and the arteries.[2]

Nonchemical Therapy

Certain drugs have been successfully used in treating hypertension and the admonition to the hypertensive is, "Stay on your medicine." Rather unfortunately, a large proportion of sufferers from hypertension do not do this. As we have already noted, hypertension is often free from symptoms and in this case there is nothing to remind the hypertensive of the importance of staying with his medication.

Even if medication is successful at controlling the condition, no one knows what will be the outcome of someone taking certain types of medicine for say, thirty-five years. One specialist in hypertension was asked about a medication of which it was said, "There were no side effects." His answer was sure and certain, "There is no such medicine."

Cost is no little consideration in the medication issue. Visits to the doctor's offices don't come cheaply anymore and when they are on a regular basis the cost really mounts up. One hypertensive going abroad for a couple of months decided to lay in a supply of pills and was a little jolted when informed the jar would cost sixty dollars.

For many, too, there comes the feeling of being dependent on chemicals. We find ourselves back again with the old idea of, "Sit still and take a pill." Many a victim of this disease asks himself if there isn't some way to take over his own life again and remembers the premise of holistic medicine, that a patient should be responsible for his own health.

What can a hypertensive do? Is he to become the passive victim of a relentless master who holds him in its grip?

Here are five decisive motivational actions you, as a hypertensive, can take:

1. *If obese, reduce your weight.* As your body weight increases it generally brings with it an increase in blood pressure. Fatty tissue, like any other tissue, must have blood and it has been estimated that each pound of fat requires a mile of capillaries to feed it. Reduce your weight ten pounds and your heart has *ten miles* less through which to push blood.

In America we are cursed with a national pastime—recreational eating. The businessman's lunch, generally on the expense account, is the place where business is allegedly done, but in reality is an activity in which impressions are made. The first step in building friendships is to have people over for a meal. Eating has become such an integral part of church life that many a church has a kitchen that a good-sized restaurant would be proud to own.

As two authorities see it, "Extra weight is so dangerous that one insurance company has estimated that a man subtracts two years from his life for every inch his waist is bigger than his chest."[3] Obesity is certainly a vital factor in the problem of hypertension. In a noteworthy study carried out in Massachusetts, the people with blood-pressure problems were found to be more obese than people with normal blood pressure. Another study carried out in men who qualified for Naval flight training showed that obesity was a major factor in those who became hypertensive.

The major step in the plan of the hypertensive then is to lose weight. This will be difficult, but it is one of the things which you can control and stop the process of digging your grave with your own knife and fork.

2. *Reduce your salt intake.* All the evidence points toward salt as a villain in the drama of hypertension. At one time the

reduction of salt was the basic strategy in treatment, but because of the high level of salt in our national diet and the use of diuretic drugs, it is sometimes claimed that it has become an archaic method of treatment. Nevertheless, it makes sense to reduce salt intake.

3. *Quit smoking.* The link of smoking with lung cancer, chronic bronchitis, and emphysema has been well-established as has cancer of the larynx, esophagus, and the bladder. Evidence is mounting to indicate cigarette smoking as the most important single additive for increasing the risk of heart attack in hypertension.

4. *Undertake a program of exercise.* Extensive studies have shown exercise to be of value in keeping blood pressure at acceptable levels and also a factor in reducing blood pressure. In one experiment at the San Diego State College exercise laboratory, twenty-three hypertensive men were involved in a program of moderate exercise—fifteen to twenty minutes warm-up calisthenics plus thirty-five minutes of walking and jogging twice a week. Emerging results showed an average drop of thirteen points on their systolic and twelve points on the diastolic measurements of their blood pressure.

Research evidence seems to show that as little as three sessions a week, lasting no more than thirty minutes a session, can produce measurable results. The action of exercise is so important that we will later give a whole chapter to its discussion and will learn something of its pervasive benefits in all areas of life.

5. *Face the factor of guilt.* A recent book was published under the title of *Sex Can Save Your Life.* The author, in an effort to bolster his case, faced the reports of men who had succumbed to a heart attack while engaged in sexual relations. Examining the cases the doctor, who is determined that sex should be looked upon as a recreational, therapeutic

activity, pointed out the main problem in the cases where sex had brought on a heart attack was that the reporters had overlooked the fact that such sexual activity was not between husband and wife. It was illicit and factors other than physical entered into the situation.

The point the writer unwittingly made was that guilt may be a significant factor in stress. The word *guilt* literally means "to pay," and a guilty person will often undergo certain physiological changes which come from his conscience or value system. If guilt is not dealt with, stress may result.

In this situation steps should be taken to manage the guilt. These would include accepting responsibility for irresponsible behavior, abandoning secrecy about the behavior and becoming open with significant others, and undertaking a plan of restitution for putting things right. All of this will serve to bring an alleviation of guilt, but ultimately guilt has to do with God and must be forgiven by him.

The Accomplice

The silent killer, hypertension, has an accomplice who is the vital force in this dirty work in undermining and sabotaging the circulatory system. Its name is stress. It has been highly successful. Hypertension is so widespread that 15 to 30 percent of the population suffer from it. One study states that diseases resulting from hypertension are responsible for two deaths every minute in the United States alone. Small wonder hypertension has been called the "hidden epidemic" and this hidden epidemic has been fueled by stress. One of the most viable ways of helping the hypertensive is to reduce stress, a subject we'll address in the following chapters. But this saboteur called stress makes many subtle approaches to our vulnerable bodies.

Workers in the health field are being forced to the conclusion that many of the symptoms seen in patients today may be the product of stress. Some of these would include such things as stomachaches, sleeplessness, chronic fatigue, constipation, and diarrhea; illnesses which do not necessarily kill, but may make life miserable. They have also noted that many of the more serious illnesses such as ulcers, asthma, and arthritis may be aggravated by stressful conditions.

What is probably the most devastating and greatly feared of all the attacks on the human body, cancer, may not be as entirely physical as we are tempted to think. At first view it seems highly improbable that such a psychological factor as stress would play a part in the development of cancer, yet there are reputable researchers who are concluding that this is so.

Some very careful research has produced verifiable evidence indicating the relationship of stress and the development of tumors. This has been particularly startling in work with animals. One researcher showed that by varying stress on mice he could alter the incidence of breast cancer from 92 percent under stressful conditions to 7 percent in a protected environment. Work such as this has been so conclusive that in the 1960s it was concluded that "no further animal experimentation delineating the relationship between stress and malignancy in laboratory animals was necessary."[4] From this we can conclude that the case is very clear as to the role of stress in developing malignancies.

All of this evidence being as convincing as it undoubtedly is, we must give our attention to dealing with stress, handling it in the first place, and then reducing it in people who are manifesting stress symptoms.

6
The Healing Potential

We have already noted the *flight or fight* mechanism within the body. This instinctive reaction is a manifestation of the body's drive to protect itself. In modern times it has become like some overloaded mechanism which is malfunctioning and gives rise to stress. Our remarkable bodies have other protective mechanisms within them which are theorotically available if we can only turn their powers loose. It becomes increasingly clear that many of these healing and creative powers may be available for us if we can just find the way to facilitate them.

It has long been known that certain forms of life, lizards, starfish, and salamanders, have the remarkable capacity to regrow a portion of their body that has been damaged. Chop off a lizard's tail and it will grow a new one in a remarkably short period of time. Speculation has often centered on the capacities resident in the bodies of human beings and the question as to whether there are regenerative powers available within our bodies. The answer seems to be that there are such forces and we may have to spend more time discovering how these powers can be mobilized.

Two thought-provoking cases have been reported recently. One concerns what has come to be referred to as "Born-again spleens." A team of medical researchers from Yale University examined twenty-two people whose spleens had been removed following childhood accidents. Tests revealed that in thirteen of these patients the filtering processes normally carried on by the spleen had continued even though that organ had been removed from one to eight years previously. The doctors concluded that cells from the ruptured organ had apparently become implanted in the walls of the abdominal cavity and developed into the clusters of what they called "mini-spleens."[1]

News from England tells of the experience of a British doctor specializing in emergency medicine and her discovery of regenerative powers of the human body. She discovered that children's fingers which had been severed as far down as the first joint could best be treated by letting the body use its own powers of healing by cleaning the wound and covering it with a bandage. Left in this state, the fingertip, including the nail, grew back in a twelve-week period. Researchers lay down three conditions: the child must be under twelve years, the cut must be above the crease in the finger, the surgeons must not interfere. The latter statement may be a reminder to us that the body has healing powers that need to be turned loose and some of our well-intentioned scientific efforts might not be so good.[2]

One doctor, a clinical professor in a highly respected medical school, is using hypnosis in the treatment of burns. He describes his theory: "A major part of a burn is really the reaction of the central nervous system to heat. The mind sends out a message and the body responds. In the case of a burn, it's an inflammatory response. Consider it in slow motion, with a sunburn. When you first leave the sun, you're generally all right. It's only in the next eight hours that the swelling, pain, fever, and blisters develop.

"If, in the first two hours after a normal burn, the person imagines that he wasn't burned, then he doesn't react."[3]

Once we have accepted the possibility that the body has regenerative powers, the next question is whether it might be possible consciously to utilize some of these powers. A goodly number of researchers have produced evidence to show that by the use of suggestion techniques it might be possible to affect the blood flow to the skin and to other areas of the body.

These experimenters utilized suggestive techniques (hypnosis being prominent among these) by which they were able to produce blisters, remove warts, reduce fishskin disease, and even to the enlarging of women's breasts. While most of these experiments were not by any means uniformly successful, the significant number of instances in which they were successful showed that something had happened in this process.

One underlying factor in each of these studies was the blood flow. One researcher reported, "Changes in the blood flow and blood volume may be part of the meditating mechanisms that produce the phenomena."[4]

A small mountain town where I lived had been the scene of extensive gold diggings in earlier days. To get the water required for washing the precious metal from the soil, it was necessary to build what were called "races" around the mountainside. The race was a carefully constructed trench which followed the contours of the mountainside and was painstakingly graded and directed to keep the water moving at the right speed and make it available at the various points where the gold could be recovered. The question is whether it would be similarly possible to plan to deliberately make blood available to specific parts of the body, not only to heal the skin but to keep the precious fluid moving through the blood vessels at the proper speed.

Most of us have long been aware of the manner in which blood flow responds to emotion. I once worked with a woman to whom I would say, "Connie, you are blushing," and her face would immediately turn to a flaming red. Her very fear of blushing triggered the process. In everyday experience anger is associated with a red face, as an increased blood supply is routed to the skin of the face, or fear, as when an individual is frightened and a pale countenance bears mute testimony to the fear. These experiences have been recognized as involuntary responses. Now has come a realization that the flow of blood routed by the emotions may in some measure be brought under the voluntary control of the will.

Some of the most promising work in voluntarily controlling blood flow has been done in connection with biofeedback machines. Biofeedback is a process by which it is possible to measure what is occurring in the body or on the skin surface. It is possible to measure such things as certain brain waves, muscular tension, and skin temperature. The skin temperature experiments are particularly relevant to the possibility of the control of blood flow. Subjects are trained in ways of controlling the flow of blood and so raising skin temperature. Many of these studies have shown that subjects can be trained to raise and lower skin temperature by as much as seven degrees. So has come measurable evidence that it is possible to voluntarily control blood flow.

The best illustration of both the function of blood flow and also its voluntary control is to be seen in the sexual response. As an individual, male or female, is sexually stimulated blood flows to one part of the body, the genitals which are engorged in readiness for sexual congress. Not only is this experience closely related to blood flow and temperature change in the genital areas but the process is intimately related to thoughts, images, imaginings, and feelings. These mental and emotional processes are the means by which the blood flow and, consequently, the shape and function of these parts of the body are changed.

In male-female relations the blood flow is regulated by the thought processes. A male is sexually responsive to a female he perceives as attractive. A female, similarly, has a bodily response commensurate with the way she views a male. Changes in the body are brought about by thoughts and feelings.

The changes can be made to come about voluntarily, and they can also be prevented by a deliberate act of the will. Counseling with young people about the problems of sexual temptation we often tell them, "Resist sexual temptation," and this involves a change of the thought processes. The counsel frequently given is in a statement attributed to Martin Luther, "You cannot stop the birds flying over your head but you can prevent them building their nests in your hair." This process involves changing the cognitive processes by turning the thoughts in the mind in another direction.

Preeminently sexual blood flow direction is related to the imaging process. A major factor in sexual response is the use of the imagination, a factor on which the pornographers do not hesitate to capitalize. Masturbation frequently involves imaging in the form of fantasy. Sex therapists working with a partner in marriage may advise the deliberate use of fantasy in the relationship to facilitate the sexual response. The subject is given instructions as to what to think.

The all-important point for our discussion is that in the human sexual response blood flow and change in organs can be controlled by thoughts, feelings, and imaging. Such a capacity may possibly be an indication of the potentiality for changes in other parts of the body by purely mental processes such as imaging, thinking, and feeling.

All this evidence indicates there are powers of growth and healing in the body that are not normally utilized. There are also some clues which indicate that the thought processes may be used to stimulate these growth capabilities. Our major problem will be to discover the way in which these powers can be developed. The Bible speaks about some of these as in Proverbs, "A merry heart doeth good like a medicine: but a broken spirit drieth the bones" (17:22); and it brings the news of the possibility of the experience of praying, "They that wait upon the Lord shall renew their strength" (Isa. 40:31). Our problem is to discover the techniques by which we can utilize the powers latent within us, a subject I will treat in subsequent chapters.

7
Christian Healing Resources

News out of recently reopened China is that—despite the rampages of the Red Guards in 1966 when Bibles were burned, Christians were killed and tortured if they did not renounce their faith, and church buildings destroyed or turned into warehouses—the church still lives in China. One reporter trying to understand how the church has managed to exist and, in some instances, flourish, stated, "Numbers grew swiftly, especially after reports that physical and mental illness were cured by prayer."[1] Healing is such a part of the church in China that it is seen as an evidence of its supernatural origin by a population steeped in atheism.

For many years chaplains in the Australian Army wore a Maltese cross as the insignia on their uniform. The insignia dated back to the day of the Crusades, when the Knights Templars established hospitals on the island of Malta to minister to the pilgrims falling ill or wounded while making their way to Palestine. The religious convictions of these soldier monks were manifested in their care of the sick. Religion has always had a close association with the sick, as is seen in the establishment of hospitals by the church, a practice which continues to this day.

It is impossible to read the Bible without becoming aware of the healing processes associated with religion. Healing was practiced in a restricted way in the Old Testament but some of the most dramatic healing miracles are to be found

69

within its pages. With the dawn of New Testament times and the ministry of Jesus there came a blaze of healing activity.

"Psychosomatic" is a word of fairly recent origin. Literally, it means "soul and body," referring to the close relationship of body and spirit. The soul affects the body, and the health of the soul may be an indication of the health of the body. In Bible times John wished for his friend Gaius, "Above all things that thou mayest prosper and be in health, even as thy soul prospereth" (3 John 2). This was an anticipation of the emphasis of psychosomatic medicine. Man is a unity; body and soul cannot be separated. Religion and health are inextricably intertwined.

There is no doubt about the close relationship of religion and healing, or about the commandment of Jesus to heal, or of the important role of the church in ministering to people in their sickness. The question to be faced is the way in which this ministry is carried on. The command of Jesus to "heal the sick" has been interpreted in a number of different ways. These include the use of suggestion, healing objects, laying on of hands, the healing campaign, praying, and the church-related hospital.

Suggestion

Weatherhead[2] has classified the healing miracles of Jesus into three categories: (1) those miracles in which suggestion seems to be the main mechanism concerned; (2) the miracles in which Christ used a more complicated technique; (3) healings in which the mental attitude of friends or bystanders produced a psychic atmosphere in which Christ could more powerfully work. Weatherhead does not claim to explain the healing miracles of Christ but only shows that they may be seen as illustrations of psychological laws and these laws he sees to be varieties of suggestion.

Suggestion has been defined as, "the uncritical acceptance of an idea" and is sometimes classified into (1) heterosuggestion, suggestion given by another; (2) contrasuggestion, a response opposite to that suggested; and (3) autosuggestion, which is defined as, "suggestion arising from oneself." Emile Coué[3] (1857-1926) was the outstanding exponent of autosuggestion. He gave his subjects the instruction, "Say every morning and evening, 'Every day, in every way I am getting better and better,' " adding with unconscious humor, "Don't think of what you are saying. Say it as you would say the litany at church." The phrase could be modified to suit individuals, but there were some stipulations. There must be no negatives; the disease must not be mentioned, for the unconscious would snatch at the name; no future tenses were to be used as it was to happen immediately. The will was not to be called into action.

There were no conscious attempts to use religion, but some of Coué's techniques, such as counting twenty knots on a piece of string while monotonously repeating, "Every day in every respect I am getting better and better," had at least some religious overtones evoking memories of the rosary. Coué's disciple, C. Harry Brooks, added an adaptation for those subjects with religious convictions and suggested that the formula might be, "Day by day, in every way, by the help of God, I'm getting better and better." He added, "It is possible that the attention of the unconscious will thus be turned to moral and spiritual improvements to a greater extent than by the ordinary formula."

The way the medical profession sometimes used placebos,

sugar pills which are implied to have medicinal value, is an illustration of the power of suggestion which will be an element in all types of healing.

Healing Objects

The story is told about an early experience in the use of the clinical thermometer with a patient who had never previously seen such a gadget. The doctor sat the patient down and placed the thermometer in his mouth. When he later returned to remove the instrument, the patient told the doctor how much the new treatment had helped him and how that he could already feel improvement in his condition. The doctor quickly caught on and gave the patient a series of treatments which consisted of having the patient sit with the thermometer in his mouth.

A modern display at a medical convention of the strange objects sold by quacks, for use by their patients, is only the extension of an age-old practice of having faith in the therapeutic powers of articles, as widely removed from each other as red flannel and electric machines. It is small wonder that religion became involved with objects somewhere along the line.

The Catholic Church has placed its blessing upon certain objects which are conceived of as enhancing faith and bringing healing. The stream of Lourdes in France, where a French girl claimed to see a vision of the virgin Mary in 1858, has become famous for its miracles and healings. Lourdes has attained such a reputation that millions of people have made the journey there to pray, bathe, and drink the waters. In a strange mixture of faith and science, great care is taken in recognizing "cures" and exhaustive inquiries are made before a "cure" is announced.

Protestants have not been immune from the use of objects. One well-known healer holds up his hand before the television screen and calls upon his viewers to place their hands on the TV set and "make contact" with the healing power. When on radio, he asks those who would be healed to touch the radio set. Some radio preachers ask their listeners to send for a "healing cloth," plus a small donation, of course. They claim that the cloth will bring healing to the listener.

It should be noted that the intrinsic value of the object in which the individual has faith is not nearly as important as the attitude of the seeker of healing. The intensity of his expectancy is apparently the determinative factor in the experience.

Laying on of Hands

The laying on of hands is one of the oldest methods of healing. Used by Christ in his ministry, the practice has become a part of the various ceremonies of the Christian church. Roman Catholics and Episcopalians see in it the symbol of apostolic succession. Some nonliturgical churches use the laying on of hands in ordaining ministers and deacons.

Belief in the healing power of the touch goes back to the dawn of history. An ancient Egyptian papyrus earlier than 1500 BC tells of healing ceremonies which involved the laying on of hands. In England it was touching by the king, who touched them while his chaplain intoned, "He put his hands on them and healed them." The custom was passed on by the royal line. King Charles II is said to have touched nearly a hundred thousand people. Queen Anne was the last of the British rulers to practice the "king's touch." One of the celebrated people she touched was the infant Samuel Johnson in

1712. James Boswell, in his *Life of Samuel Johnson,* tells us that Johnson's mother took him to be "touched" on the advice of the family physician, but it was all to no avail, as he was not healed.

The custom spread to the Continent and was practiced by many of the French kings. Not all rulers were convinced, however, and it is recorded that William of Orange considered the practice a mere superstition, and he only touched one person. During the process, he muttered, "May God give you better health and more sense."

Faith healers who specialize in healing campaigns generally lay hands on their subjects. They frequently boast about their "healing right arm" and the feeling, like an electric shock, which comes from it.

I once served as the chaplain of a large army hospital where we had a fine dermatologist of Polish origin and training. While on rounds with him one day, we stopped before a bad case of dermatitis. The nurse removed the dressings to show the badly infected skin. Without a moment's hesitation the dedicated doctor leaned over and began to rub his fingers over the infected spots. The onlookers were amazed, as was the patient. Smiling into the patient's face, the dermatologist assured him that everything was going to be all right. Back in his office later, I asked the doctor if it was his usual practice to touch the infected spots. He replied that in his medical training he had been taught never to show fear in the presence of infection. It was claimed that a confident attitude helped to quell the apprehensions of the patient. It could be that the contact of laying on hands has a value of breaking down the isolation which sickness sometimes brings.

Weatherhead[4] gives a limited endorsement to the practice of laying on of hands but suggests precautions which should be observed. (1) The laying on of hands should take place in private. (2) It should not be indicated that this can replace adequate medical diagnosis and treatment. (3) The minister should be a dedicated person who sees himself as representing the whole church in his action.

The Healing Campaign

A large hall is packed with people, and the song leader directs in the swinging, stirring songs, now and then referring to Brother Jones who will later bring the message of the evening. At a climactic moment, Brother Jones appears on the platform. In appearance more like a wrestler than a preacher, he is snappily dressed and begins to preach in a rapid-fire manner. He tells how an angel appeared to him in a dream with the news that he was to receive the gift of healing, and from that moment on God has performed miraculous healings through him. He explains what happens within him. A feeling comes in the pit of his stomach, then rises through his body and into his arms. It is happening now. It is just like electricity tingling in his right arm. When you come forward and he lays hands on you, you will feel the tingling sensation. Of course, you may not feel it, but it will happen just the same.

The speaker takes some time to carefully explain there are two things that can happen. It will be either a healing or a miracle. If it is a miracle, it will take place immediately, but if it is a healing it may take longer, as a slow, gradual process. He is also careful to point out that it is faith that does it. Only a lack of faith will prevent a healing.

A healing line is formed. Only those who have been previously interviewed and given cards are allowed to queue up. Critics say that it is a screening process to make sure that only those with functional illnesses come. A man leads the line across the platform. Brother Jones asks if he believes Jesus can heal him, and when he responds in the affirmative, the preacher smears some oil on his forehead, presses his hands down on his head, and prays in a loud voice, "Lord, remove this demon from this man, heal, heal, in the name of Jesus of Nazareth, come out of him thou deaf demon, come out of him!" Jones makes a strange hissing noise, "Sh . . . sh," and exclaims, "There it goes, it has gone." Turning to the bewildered subject, he says, "You are healed now aren't you?" The man nods.

"Say 'Thank you, Jesus.' "

The subject stutters, "Thank you, Jesus."

The healer turns to the crowd and says, "Give Jesus a big hand," and the audience joins in the applause.

After a few dramatic healings, the healer begins to tire. He announces that he is feeling in his body all the ailments of those who come to him, and it will not be possible for him to continue any longer. A murmur of disappointment goes down the healing line as Brother Jones disappears from the platform, and is spirited away so that no one can talk with him.

We have been eyewitnesses to a meeting in connection with a healing campaign which is a common occurrence across the nation. Often with enormous tents and a strange assortment of electronic gear, the healers move in on a town and become the spotlight of attention. Claims go to ridiculous extremes. One pamphlet distributed by a healer shows a boy with a plastic eye in his hand. The boy had lost his eye and now wore an artificial one. After attending a healing service, he was able to see through the plastic eye. Such claims attract a large following, and one healer is reported to have programs on 233 radio and 95 television stations.

Healers claim to be fulfilling the command of Jesus to heal, and many people give testimony to the veracity of their assertions. Can it be that this is the authentic healing activity of which the New Testament speaks? An examination of the situation leads the impartial observer to reject the claims for a number of reasons.

Although testimonies to healing are often heard, there is very little evidence produced to verify the fact. Cases reported are not accompanied by case histories which a medical examiner would require. The Roman Catholic shrine at Lourdes requires a medical examination before the sick person visits the shrine, another after the healing is claimed, a further medical report from the home doctor twelve months later, and then on returning to the shrine, a reexamination by three doctors. Even with all this care, there have been some fraudulent claims. Most leaders of healing campaigns are not willing to have their cases investigated and will frequently become very hostile if an investigation is attempted. Consequently, the possibility of deception is great.

Everything in the healing campaign is geared toward raising suggestibility. The careful build-up of the reputation of the healer, the highly emotionalized responses of the crowds, the emphasis on the subject having faith, the apparent "miracles" taking place, all create the climate of anticipation. One psychiatrist noted the glassy eyes of the subjects and saw evidence of a hypnotic trance. In the suggestible atmosphere the symptom is removed, and the crowd is informed that the subject is healed. One can well imagine the awful disappointment when later the symptom reappears or is replaced by another. One observer noted the number of "repeaters" who were to be found in the healing line. Apparently addicted to it, they had to come periodically to have their symptoms removed.

There is religious as well as psychological confusion in the healing campaign. The healers claim that they are carrying on the healing activity of Jesus, but there is no biblical sanction for the healing campaign in which everything is done with an eye to publicity. One healer stated, "There is no such thing as bad publicity; even when it is bad, it is good." Contrast this with Jesus who urged those who were healed to "tell no man."

The nature of faith is misrepresented. It is claimed that if the subject has faith he will be healed and that if he is not healed it will be because of a lack of faith. Very often stable, well-balanced people are not healed, while neurotic, shallow individuals with a very immature faith have miraculous experiences. Possibly the worst aspect of it is the impression that God is a means to man's end. One faith healer says, "Our faith makes God act." This statement shows his belief in magic rather than a mature faith. No well-informed Christian would dare to make God a means to man's end. Man must always be a means to God's end.

The Church-Related Hospital

One effort to fulfill Christ's command to "heal the sick" has been seen in the establishment of church-related hospitals. The rationale is that God guides the scientists in their research and may be working through the medical research that goes into the making of a hospital. Wherever missionaries have gone, hospitals have almost inevitably followed and church-related hospitals dot the American countryside.

Rather unfortunately, once the hospital has been established the distinctive Christian note is frequently lost. Institutions have a strange tendency to gain a momentum in their own right and guided by the professionals in the field who may have administrative skills, medical knowledge, or research capacities, but few religious convictions. A goodly proportion of church-related hospitals have become completely secularized, the only concession to their origin being in some instances a chaplain's department. Frequently this department is an appendage rather like the appendix, a vestige of early development which is seen as completely unnecessary now.

So has come the strange anomaly that the very place where the ministry of praying for the sick should be found in its most highly developed form there frequently isn't too much praying done. Where the hospital does happen to have a chaplain's department, many of the chaplains in these settings are often more interested in psychology than in religion and have been so much influenced by their secular scientific fellow workers that they do not consider praying with people to be one of their major responsibilities. While undergoing a hospital stay in a church-related institution, I was visited by a number of staff members from the chaplain's department. Not one of them ever offered to pray with me. Visiting and counseling with patients were apparently important, but praying?

The church-related hospital may be a commendable exercise in altruism, an effort to ameliorate the sufferings of mankind, but as an effort to promote religious healing utilizing spiritual resources they have been notable failures.

Prayer

Some years ago a survey was made of ministries asking if they had ever attempted a spiritual healing. Nearly half of them reported having been involved in such an experience. When asked what method of healing they preferred, most named prayer as the favored method. There can be no doubt that prayer has always been recognized as the primary vehicle for spiritual healing. The major question is how will prayer be utilized.

Other factors enter to complicate the use of prayer in sickness. It may be in part because of the Catholic practice of administering the last rites to the dying, but some people are not overly enthusiastic about prayers being offered over them when they are sick. I once told a church member who was entering the hospital for surgery that I'd come by to see him just before the operation. He looked at me and said, "Please don't come praying over me. It gives me the feeling that I might die."

Years later, by a strange coincidence, I looked into the same man's face across the bed of his dying wife. I asked, "Shall I pray now?"

His eyes flooded with tears and he responded, "Please do."

Will others pray for the sick individual?

Many churches have what is sometimes referred to by the not-so-pious as "sick call." The order is that the pastor reads the names of the sick. Incidentally, one main virtue of this practice seems to be giving the information about the health of certain people. After this reading he or someone else will pray for the sick and beseech the Lord to "lay his hands of healing upon them." In such a meeting there is little effort to involve the whole company assembled.

Some churches have attempted to improve this by breaking into small groups where a large number of people can participate. Another technique is to present each sick person's name individually to the assembled company. The leader calls upon the group to focus their prayer interest on this person with each petitioner visualizing the sick one on the screen of his or her mind. This type of praying seems to offer a tremendous potentiality for really fulfilling the admonition of praying for the sick.

The prayer of faith may represent an important part of a cooperative attempt to minister to the sick person. Believing God is at work in medical discoveries, we can see God's healing hand mediated through the medical profession. Add to this the element of the prayer of faith and we have an ideal combination. An apparently healthy woman was told by her doctor she had a malignant growth and surgery was proposed. She went to her pastor who encouraged her to proceed with the surgery. Then he called together a group of like-minded people from the church. They gathered at the woman's home and prayed over her. The surgery was successful. What had healed her? Surgery? Prayer? Both?

Another prayer possibility is for one to pray for oneself. This type of praying has t010mdous potential which we will examine in a later chapter.

Part II
A Plan for Defusing
the Time Bomb

8
Adopt a Stress-Coping Life-Style

We have noted earlier that some occupations are apparently more stressful than others. One that comes most readily to mind is that of air traffic controller. Research has shown that in some situations an air traffic controller's blood pressure may shoot up as much as fifty points, providing what has been called a textbook example of psychological stress. Such stress would seem to indicate that people working in these situations would be more prone to heart attacks and strokes than the average citizens. The startling discovery is that they are not, and in many areas they are actually much healthier than the rest of the population.[1]

Another study of people who had been through what must have been the most stressful of all life situations—Nazi concentration camps—showed that one fourth of them gave no indication of stress-related conditions after their release. These two groups, Nazi concentration camp victims and air traffic controllers, may remind us that it is not so much the stress of the situations as it is the attitude of the subjects to the stressors.

One response to the stress problem has been the use of chemicals. The most widely prescribed drug in America today is the tranquilizer valium. Conducting an investigation into the use of valium, a Senate health subcommittee turned up some alarming evidence that the cure might be worse than the disease. One member stated, "Tranquilizing of America has become very big business. The experts who treat drug and alcohol addiction . . . see this as a growing and very serious public health problem."

Some of the evidence heard by this Senate committee helped to confirm the apprehensions of this member. A psychiatrist, pointing an accusing finger at the pharmaceutical companies, told of the unending stream of free samples coming in the doctor's mail and their effects. He said, "When other doctors read their mail I ate mine." One expert testified, "I see patients with detectable withdrawal syndrome who have taken the drug (valium) for periods as short as five or six weeks." One Atlanta doctor stated that withdrawal from valium, "is more prolonged and often more difficult than withdrawal from heroin." With doctors writing more than forty-four million prescriptions for valium in one year the problem is assuming monumental proportions. The difficulty lies in Americans believing that salvation lies in a pill. As Dr. Pusch puts it, "These drugs make people feel better because they make them feel dull and insensitive. But they don't solve anything."[2]

Our propensity towards taking medicine is a sad commentary on one of humanity's most vulnerable points. Sir William Osler once said, "The human species is distinguished from the lower orders by its desire to take medicine." Rather unfortunately the use of drugs to cope with stress is of doubtful value. At its best, a drug is a crutch to help the subject over a rough spot, but if used too freely the user may never get up onto his own two feet again.

Putting Balance into Life

Many elements go into the making of life and each of these elements plays a part in determining how we handle the ever-

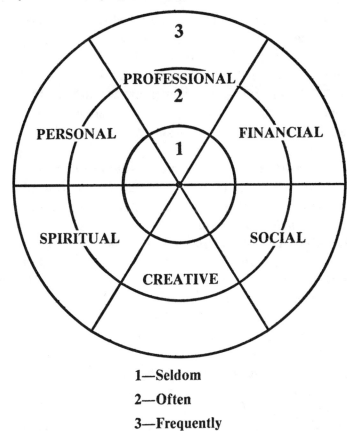

1—Seldom

2—Often

3—Frequently

changing situations we face from day to day. One way of doing this is to see your life as a flywheel made up of a number of elements. The function of a flywheel in engines is two-fold. The first is to smooth out irregular running. This is particularly so in an internal-combustion engine where the periodic explosive force would cause an irregular running but the flywheel absorbs the excess energy and lets it run smooth-ly. A second function is to provide momentum which keeps the engine moving when there is no power available. This momentum is really stored up energy which is provided by the flywheel.

The flywheel of life can similarly be seen to fulfill a like function in human personality. It can make life smooth or rough and can provide the momentum we all need to keep life moving through its widely varied experiences. The flywheel of life is made up of six segments.

PROFESSIONAL, *which represents the central activity by which an individual earns his living. The satisfaction it brings can vary widely. Work can be a joy or a drudgery. Ideally, it ought to be fulfilling.*

FINANCIAL, *an area that provides the economic underpinnings of an individual's existence. It may be seen in the size of the paycheck, the way money is earned, and certainly in the way an individual goes about spending it.*

SOCIAL, *being the relationships an individual has with other people, family, friends, associates, and significant people of the opposite sex.*

SPIRITUAL, *the activities which give one a sense of relationship with God, a sense of mission in life, a divine plan, and a sense of destiny.*

CREATIVE, *activities which give a person a feeling of accomplishment and a way of expressing his own uniqueness.*

PERSONAL, *which involves an individual's sense of his own personal worth and well-being which comes from an adequate diet, a good exercise program, meaningful relaxation, and times of privacy.*

Look now at the flywheel of life and make it into an expression of your own life. Shade off each of the segments.

Begin from the center and work out. Try to make a subjective evaluation of yourself in each of these six areas.

How does it look?

Let's go back to the flywheel concept. Imagine the flywheel in which the weight of the wheel is distributed in the same manner as your personal attributes appear on the wheel of life. Is your wheel lumpy or uneven? How big is your wheel? Do you need to set some new goals about taking some positive action?

All of this has direct application to the stress problem. Albrecht, in his discussion of the low stress life-style, suggests that the two major principles for living like this are balance and adaptation. Balance would be in keeping a sense of proportion in the six segments of the flywheel of life. Adaptation is the ability to take things in one's psychological stride. This person can keep life's momentum going which is the function of the flywheel of life.

A Plan for Coping

Some of the viable methods of coping with stress would include the following:

- Plan your day so you will have a realistic idea as to what time you have and what you can accomplish. At the beginning of the day write out a "to do" list and check off each chore as it is finished. Let those that are left over be the basis for your next day's "to do."
- Avoid the temptation to withdraw and stew over your problems. Move toward, not away from people. Join a share group within which you can learn to overcome your tendencies to withdraw.
- Overcome your tendency to procrastinate. Don't put things off. Do the unpleasant things first. Resist the

temptation to leave them hanging over your head.

- Remember who you are mad at. When you are upset or feel uneasy, sit down and think about what went into the making of the situation. Realistically face the source of your stress.

- Overcome your sense of omnipotence. You are not God, at your best you are his servant. Forget about being a superman. Realize your own limitations and work within them.

- Learn to say no on occasions. When family or friends or employees make abnormal demands on you, just politely say, "I'm sorry, as much as I would like to, I cannot do it." Don't feel guilty, you are entitled to say no.

- Remember how to eat an elephant. The task often looks so big it seems impossible. Start in on one portion, one that you can manage, then leave it for a little while, come back again. Once you get a part of it done the rest will seem easier. To eat an elephant, you take one bite at a time.

- Give the other person a break. If you are highly motivated, you may be driven by a desire to always win. Let someone else win occasionally. It won't hurt you and that person will probably feel better about you.

- Face the fact there are some things that you cannot change. Spend some time with the Serenity Prayer. "God grant me the serenity to accept the things I cannot change, courage to change things I can, and wisdom to know the difference."

- Embark on a long-range program for defusing the time bomb within—as set out in the following chapters.

9
Move and Really Live

The fight or flight mechanism within human personality is a reminder that humans are built to deal physically with the problems they face in life. When the fight or flight mechanism takes over, the individual is geared up and ready to move into physical action. But, as we have already noted, direct physical action is generally inappropriate. We cannot attack or turn our back on the boss when he has annoyed us. All we can do is present a smiling face and stew inside.

But there are physical things we can do which may offer us one of the most effective tools for dealing with stress. The recognition is gradually coming that, although at first glance it seems unrelated to how we feel, exercise may be a significant factor in dealing with emotions.

Lawrence LeShan[1] has suggested that as unlikely as it seems, a program of meditation and a program of exercise have many things in common. Both call for hard application to the task. In many programs of exercise the main enemy is boredom and it takes a strong-minded person to stay with a regular exercise program. The highway of physical fitness is littered with dropouts. Similarly with meditation techniques, most people just don't have enough drive to use them consistently. Like exercise, meditation can often seem to be a somewhat foolish activity. What could be more ridiculous than running in place, lifting a heavy object up and down for long periods of time, or riding a stationary bicycle to nowhere? Perhaps the closest rival would be the rather ordinary repetitions that are so much a part of meditation techniques. The simple repetitious nature of both exercise and meditation leaves them open to the criticism that they are oversimplified techniques.

Then there is the secondary goal coming from primary activity. Both meditation and exercise are geared toward training the individual in preparation for moving toward an ultimate goal. They are never seen to be an end in themselves and for this reason it is frequently hard to see a future in them. Still further, both exercise and meditation are highly individual matters. In both of these types of programs, to be effective they must be tailored to the individual and, rather unfortunately, enthusiasts in both fields have a tendency to overlook the importance of individual programs.

One man who has realized the significance of individualized exercise programs is Dr. Kenneth Cooper. He is a man with a number of credits, including that of influencing the vocabulary of a language. Just in case you get the idea that Dr. Cooper is a linguistics specialist or a writer of plays and poems, I would like to point out he is a medical doctor and the language influenced is not his native English. It seems that Cooper's ideas about the virtues of jogging caught on in South America, but they don't call it jogging. One businessman inquiring of another as to whether he has done his jogging for the day, will inquire if he has done his "Coopers" today. This addition to the language is indicative of the widespread interest in exercise programs today.

Exercise is coming to be seen as a significant factor in the emotional life of the individual. Though it would be difficult to produce hard evidence, some investigators are picking up on the old idea that the emotional states may be associated with chemical changes in the body and that these chemical levels are related to the body's activity. A professor of physical education has reported what he calls a "significant relationship" between changes in certain hormone levels in executives brought on by exercise and their emotional stability.[2] A psychiatrist has joined the physiologist in advancing the action-leading-to-chemical-change theory, seeing the brain as being subject to this change. He is presently working with researchers at the National Institute of Mental Health, inquiring into the possibilities of this theory.

The effects of exercise on mental health have been so positive that eager investigators are making enthusiastic claims. A psychiatrist has stated his conviction that mild depression is more common than the common cold but can be markedly helped by slow endurance exercise. A writer, in a burst of euphoria, has proclaimed that weekend jogging activities "could well be the basis for the nation's first grass-roots movement in community mental health."

Some mental health professionals have apparently just run upon (in more ways than one) the idea of exercise helping with emotional problems. One psychiatrist who had taken up jogging with the hope of building his own physical fitness suddenly discovered the activity might have another application. Looking at his fellow joggers, he concluded, "Nobody jogging down the track appears to be depressed." Noting that 70 percent of his patients were depressives, he quickly added exercise to his list of treatments and concluded that exercise is more effective than pills in controlling depression. He discovered that 15 to 20 percent depressives shared a quick benefit after as little as a week of running.

The body-emotions relationship helps us to get a handle on this business of emotions. Whereas in the past the sufferer often felt himself in the grip of a powerful emotional force beyond his control, he now has discovered a way to control his emotions. As E. Stanley Jones once said, "It is much easier to act yourself into a new way of feeling than to feel yourself into a new way of acting." Many of the serious exercisers are speaking about the "aerobic glow," a feeling of well-being which comes from a program of intensive exercise.

It is said that that great prober of the human psyche, Sigmund Freud, when asked which were the most important experiences of humans, responded, "Work and love." To many this seems a strange amalgam: love, the emotional, ecstatic state; work, the slogging, humdrum routine. Yet the two may have more in common than we sometimes think. Alan Alda, the highly successful actor who spends a good portion of his time working in the make-believe world of film and television, with fictional stories of love and romance, is very much a realist when he examines his own love life and twenty-three-year marriage. Asked about the nature of love Alda responded, "Love is work and work is love," and goes on to maintain that every relationship is based upon hard work. "You cannot have affection for something without working on that relationship." And so it turns out that even the experience of love, which is supposed to "conquer all," is something that calls for work and action.

The principle of action may have some wide applications to physical health. It certainly did for Norman Cousins. This outspoken author and editor found himself in the hospital diagnosed as having an arthritic condition known as Ankylosing Splondylitus. The condition was painful and the doctor gave Cousins one chance in five hundred for recovery.

Cousins decided to take matters into his own hands. He decided the actions of his body could change his pain and his feelings. He experimented by having films screened for his entertainment. They were comedies, old Marx Brothers films, and clips from *Candid Camera*. He loved them and, despite his illness, roared with laughter. He noted, "It worked . . . ten minutes of belly laughter had an anesthetic effect and would give me at least two hours of pain-free sleep."[3] Best of all, the test showed he had improved physically.

This experience, which Cousins saw as a gigantic self-administered placebo, caused the literate Cousins to put his pen to paper and write a book in which he discussed such issues as holistic medicine and the necessity of treating people over against treating diseases. Cousins sees his own case as evidence of the healing power of nature.

Movement is an indicator of life. Absence of life is shown by absence of movement and the sedentary style of life we live today may play a large part in bringing healing for many of the maladies with which we suffer. To the ideas of "fight or flight" as methods of responding to stress we may have to add planned exercise. Cousins relates a statement once made to him by Dr. Albert Schweitzer, "Each patient carries his own doctor inside him. They come to us not knowing that truth. We are at our best when we give the doctor who resides within each patient a chance to go to work." A plan of exercise may be at least a part of a therapeutic regimen, the larger element of which we will consider later.

There are a variety of ways of referring to the body of a deceased human. The more medically minded refer to it as a cadaver, which sounds rather like a reference to some other nonhuman species. An undertaker I once knew would sometimes startle a loved one by asking what they wanted done with "the remains," a statement somewhat akin to suggesting the leftovers from the meal which might be kept in the refrigerator. The vague reference to "the departed" contains at least an inference that he might just be "out for lunch." "Corpse" has a certain ominous note about it. All things being considered, for me, the most graphic, accurate, and descriptive word is the colloquialism "stiff." This word sums up the essential difference between life and death. Life means movement, complete lack of movement as indicated by the word *stiff* graphically presents death.

As a youth I spent some months in a hospital. I'd fractured my thigh and following a period in a special splint suspended from a frame over the bed with a weight extending my leg there came a long spell, still in bed, with my limb encased in a plaster cast. A ten-year-old boy in the bed next to me had a similar injury but refused to remain still as he was frequently admonished by the nurses and doctors. The day his leg was encased in plaster he inveigled an orderly into getting him a pair of crutches and sneaked outside. A week or so later he electrified the whole hospital community when a nurse espied him at the top of a thirty-foot tree with a plastered leg dangling below. Mentally I speculated that kid would come to a sticky end and finish up with a pretzel-shaped limb. But within a few months he was playing soccer while I limped to the out-patient department to have my stiffened knee manipulated and finally finished up with an arthritic condition which has returned to haunt me some thirty years later.

The boy with the broken leg is typical of many children who refuse to stay still like "good children" should. Reports come of nurses driven to distraction by small fry, recently operated on, crawling around, standing, playing games, and climbing over the end of the bed, and making remarkable recoveries.

Experiments have noted the same phenomena with animals. After some types of operations in a laboratory, an animal refuses to remain inert, gets up, wanders around, takes a few periods of rest, eating, and drinking in a normal manner. Strange as it may seem to the followers of the rest and recover regimen, the wounds from the operations heal remarkably well.

An obstreperous patient caused Dr. Daniel J. Leithauser to pay attention to the relationship of action to healing. A thirty-eight-year-old man with scant regard for medical authority, insisted on frequently leaving his bed just a few hours after the removal of his appendix, and despite warnings about possible dire results, departed from the hospital on the following day. The next day he took a thirty-mile drive into the downtown area of the city, and on the third and fourth days following his operation went to work in his garden. He followed his two days of agricultural activity by journeying forty miles on the next day to the doctor's office for an examination which showed him to be in excellent condition.

Considering this patient, the thoughtful doctor launched himself on a quest to discover the relationship between early rising and healing. Starting from the conviction that nature was the real healer, he postulated the surgeon's task was to provide the conditions under which nature could work, and concluded this could best be brought to pass by having patients rise from bed on the day of surgery. He later discovered that a certain Emil Ries of Chicago, nearly fifty years before, had undertaken a similar investigation but the insights of the pioneer researcher had not been utilized in the way that they should have. From his own research Dr. Leithauser became so convinced about the merits of patients rising from bed on the day of surgery that he declared, "It is important not because it *can* be done, but because it *must* be done." This led to his formulation, "The patient should have no choice as to early ambulation."[4]

Confirmation of the role of movement in healing has come from a number of sources. Medical researchers more than fifty years ago noted cancer was less likely to occur in the poor and the overworked than in the well-to-do and "indolent," and one of them fingered lack of exercise as a factor in the development of malignancy. During World War II, British hospitals faced with air raids and the necessity of discharging patients earlier than they normally would, discovered to their great joy that patients forced into leaving their beds earlier had a much more rapid rate of recovery.

The activity premise goes even further than this. In their discussion of the treatment of cancer by the reduction of stress, Simonton and Creighton recognize the importance of exercise as a part of their treatment regimen. They theorize that exercise brings a number of benifits to the cancer patient.

1. Exercise provides a means of handling stress by providing a physiological outlet for a response that in its original primitive form was preeminently physical.

2. A program of exercise requires planning by setting aside specific times for the activity. The patient has a sense of having taken charge of his life, being able to put things in order.

3. All the studies available seem to indicate people have a better self-concept, improved self-acceptance, a lessened

tendency to blame others, and fewer bouts of depression. This latter becomes important as the patient seems to be related to the impaired functioning of the immune system.

4. Studies seem to indicate that in some way these exercise programs stimulate the body's immunity system. Physical exercise is one of the best tools for appropriately channeling the physiological effects of stress and may also stimulate the body's natural defenses to do battle with malignancy."[5] The program suggested by Simonton and Creighton calls for at least one hour of exercise three times a week. The plan is to go at it slowly, walking around the room, lying in bed, but moving arms and legs. If this is not possible, the patient is to engage in fantasy, visualizing oneself on the screen of his or her mind as engaged in physical activity.

The very people who are apparently most susceptible to stress—business executives—are catching on to the role of exercise in reducing stress as is seen in the Tyler Cup. In this two-mile minimarathon top executives from leading companies of the nation compete against time and each other. They gather in Dallas at the Aerobics Center headed by Dr. Kenneth Cooper, whose books, example, and establishment have sent Americans and others running as they have never run before. According to the latest figures there may be as many as twenty-five million joggers in this country.

Business has also played a part in the process. The Tyler Cup awarded to the winner of this contest is named for the company that has been active in promoting jogging for executives and has led to board chairpersons, company presidents, and executive vice-presidents from such companies as Boeing, Xerox, Owens-Corning Fiberglass, TWA, Harper and Row, Readers Digest, McGraw-Hill, Citibank, and Prudential Insurance donning their shorts and shirts, pulling on their shoes, and running around the track. These people come to Dallas, Texas, to compete in the Tyler Cup, but for many of them running has become a way of life. An executive of Tyler Company puts it clearly, "We have run every place, through the lobbies of the Ritz in Paris, the Waldorf-Astoria in New York and in the best hotels in London and Geneva."

Exercise may be the closest thing we have to a panacea for the ills that beset the human frame. It is the prescription without medicine, the mood elevator without the drugs, the pickup without the hangover, the weight control without the diet, the cosmetics found in no drugstore, the sedative without a chemical, the tranquilizer without a pill, the indicator of life without a cardiogram, the therapy more effective than any psychiatrist's couch, the cure for depression without a fee, the fountain of life without a legend. At last, exercise is coming into its own. It will be an ever-increasingly important weapon in the battle against stress.

10
Find Some Friends
of the Heart

Interstate 20 stretches from Fort Worth, Texas, proudly proclaiming itself as "Where the West begins," and makes a beeline into New Mexico, passing through a very unusual stretch of West Texas countryside on the way. About seventy miles from Fort Worth the highway bisects the town of Thurber, now a ghost town, but in former years famous as a coal mining center for the Texas Pacific Railroad, producing as much as 3,000 tons of coal daily in its heyday. Replaced by the discovery of oil (Texas tea) at proximate Ranger, duly considering the energy situation, it may rise again to provide its black diamonds for an energy hungry America.

There was one shining moment in the tumultuous 60s when 300 young people settled in a group of old cabins to establish a commune amid the spinifex and stunted mesquite trees that dot the barren landscape. I spent some time investigating these kids who called themselves the Children of God.[1] As I moved among them I could not help admiring their commitment and my wife asked me the all-important question, "Are you ready to join up?"

I gazed at the broken-down cabins, the muddy pond, the bleak landscape, and responded, "I'm very attracted to them but I'm afraid I like the creature comforts too much to spend my life in these barren surroundings."

What were these kids doing here?

They were seeking experiences of affiliation and association. Being children of the 60s they had turned their backs on their biological families and some of them even misapplying the Bible by quoting the words of Jesus, "If any man . . . hate not his father, and mother, . . . he cannot be my disciple" (Luke 14:26). This religious arm of the counterculture movement, by its actions, was saying that the family spirit was displacing the biological family unit. The secular arm of the same movement, in its establishment of communes, was very specific in this by adopting names such as the Lynch family or the Jones family.

The strange contradiction of the counterculture movement, turning its back on traditional establishment ideas such as marriage, child-rearing, and family units, yet calling themselves families, might make more sense than it first appears. It may represent a recognition of the special role of family type relationships in fostering personality development.

Psychologist Lynch, in his perceptive book, *The Broken Heart—The Medical Consequences of Loneliness,* compared two states, Nevada and Utah. In location, education, and living standards, these two were almost evenly matched. Yet something strange was happening, for while Nevada has the highest death rates in the country for white males and females between the ages of twenty-five and sixty-four, contiguous Utah has one of the lowest death rates in the United States. The not-so-obvious factor is the network of relationships called the family. Nevada is one of the divorce capitals of the United States. Their next-door neighbor, Utah, with its strong Mormon influence, has only half as many divorces as Nevada. Lynch maintains that every segment of society is deeply afflicted by a major disease generally unrecognized—human loneliness.

Lynch goes on to extend his investigation in his tables of disease and death rates for both the United States of America and Japan. In the rates of death resulting from cancer non-married individuals are significantly higher. During the period 1959-61 in the ages of fifteen to sixty-four, Lynch notes, "In almost every case for both males and females, widowed, divorced, and single people have significantly higher death rates than married people."[2] Turning to the Japanese population, Lynch shows that between ages twenty and twenty-four the death rate for widowed Japanese was a whopping 31.23 times greater than their married counterparts. From his research Lynch postulates, "The lack of human companionship, the sudden loss of love, and chronic human loneliness are significant contributions to a serious disease (including cardiovascular disease) and premature death."[3]

The situation is like the proposition that used to be presented to the person who inquired as to what was the most important factor in living a long and healthy life. The proposal, "Be born of healthy parents." Following the counsel of Lynch, we know the best experience for the well-being of each of us would be to belong to a good, healthy, robust family. Where is that family?

The condition of the family in general is so bad that it has all the elements of the celebrated Gordian knot. As the Greeks told the story, Gordius, a peasant, had become the king of Phrygia and left his wagon in the town square. The yoke once used by the oxen was tied to the shaft of the wagon with a cunningly devised knot, and it was widely believed the first man to untie the knot would become the ruler of Asia. Aspirants came and went across the years until Alexander of Macedon came riding in on his fabled charger. The young nobleman struggled with the knot then petulantly stepped back, pulled out his sword, and slashed the stubborn rope and went on to the time when he is alleged to have sat down and wept because there were no worlds left to conquer.

The expression "Gordian knot" has come to be used of an apparently insoluble problem and the saying, "Slashing the Gordian knot," to refer to a drastic solution to a complex dilemma, which may have particular application to the difficulties faced by families today. One authority has uttered the dire prediction, "If the present rate of increase in divorce and single households continues to accelerate as it did for the last ten years, by mid-1990 not one American family will be left."[4]

The solution to such a problem will call for slashing the Gordian knot and the instrument with which to do it might well be NIEF (pronounced knife).

The NIEF Principle

Sociologists refer to communes as intentional families. One way to come at the problem of providing experiences of affiliation and relationship would be to set up a new entity which would include the strong points of the natural but disappearing extended family combined with the best features of the intentional family.

To be really viable this new organization which we will call the New Intentional Extended Family will have a number of features.

1. *Multigenerational—all ages from babyhood to old age.*—These people would be available for relationship experiences and be willing to become surrogate parents, children, and so forth, to those needing these relationships. This pool of people would be concerned about reaching out to welcome

others who needed experiences of affiliation and association.

2. *The group would be stable.*—In contrast to the short-lived communes, this group would have a good historic background of experience that would enable it to continue on despite the vicissitudes of the surrounding society.

3. *A central object of devotion.*—The past has shown that intentional groups which survived have a religious belief which forms a bond of union. The ideal organization would make a heavy emphasis on religious commitment. Jane Howard speaks of friends of two types, friends of the road—people we meet because of where we work, play, or live. The other type are friends of the heart—people we choose to be friends with. If friends of the heart share a common interest or commitment, the new cluster has a lot going for it.

4. *A federation rather than a union.*—The members can have the best of both worlds belonging to a biological as well as an intentional family. It would be their option that they might periodically withdraw from the intentional family to the shelter of the biological family, or if the biological family was not providing what they needed, they could then move to the closer association with the intentional family.

5. *The right to select fellow family members.*—Members of the intentional extended family would have the right to choose the people with whom they would relate. The supply would be large, so there would be many different varieties of relationships available.

6. *A wide organization.*—The ideal intentional extended family organization would be national and international. The national organization would have branches in every city and hamlet of our land.

The one organization that meets these criteria and is

uniquely suited for this task is the church. There is no institution on the face of the earth which is so suited to minister to the family as is the church. To fulfill this function the church should become the new intentional extended family of the heart.

The Benefits of Group Experiences

Life is a process of socialization. A baby born into the world alone begins a process of being introduced to people, people, people. Commencing with mother and members of the family it moves in ever-widening circles. The skill of living is the skill of relationships and as relationships are extended the growing individual builds relationships into the surrounding community.

Everybody needs a group to whom he or she can turn when life's pressures begin to mount; and some of the most successful techniques of helping people with their difficulties have been through the use of groups. Of course there are many people who object and say, "They are probably just the same as I, struggling with their own problems, how can they help me?" These types of statements are often indicators that the subject has a particular need for group experiences.

The best way to evaluate a group is to ask people about their experiences. Such a procedure was carried out some years ago when people involved in a group counseling program were asked to check the statements that most nearly expressed how they felt about their group experiences. The following were the most frequently checked responses.

Helping others has given me more self-respect.
Giving part of myself to others.

Belonging to and being accepted by a group.

Feeling alone no longer.

Learning I'm not the only one with my type of problem: "We're all in the same boat."
Seeing that I was just as well off as others.

Learning how I come across to others.
Other members honestly telling me what they think of me.

Feeling more trustful of groups and of other people.
Learning about the way I related to the other group members.

Group members suggesting or advising something for me to do.
Group members telling me what to do.

Getting things off my chest.
Learning how to express my feelings.

Admiring and behaving like my therapist.
Finding someone in the group I could pattern myself after.

Being in the group somehow helped me to understand how I grew up in my family.

Learning why I think and feel the way I do (that is, learning some of the causes and sources of my problems).
Discovering and accepting previously unknown or unacceptable parts of myself.

Seeing others getting better was inspiring to me.
Seeing that others had solved problems similar to mine.

Recognizing that life is at times unfair and unjust.
Recognizing that no matter how close I get to other people, I must still face life alone.[5]

It can readily be seen that for these participants belonging to a group had brought some very real benefits. Not only in giving help but also in clarifying some of the actions that needed to be taken. In one group the members frequently quote an aphorism which says it nicely, "We alone can do it, but we cannot do it alone."

The ultimate relationship experience is between a man and his God and no experience in socialization is ever complete until an individual is well related to God. Because divine truth is so often mediated through human personality it is frequently through relating to people that we learn to relate to God. Once rightly related with God through faith in our Lord Jesus Christ we discover a new relationship with a whole group of like-minded people.

The situation was dramatized in the ministry of Jesus:

While he yet talked to the people, behold, his mother and his brethren stood without, desiring to speak with him.

Then one said unto him, Behold, thy mother and thy brethren stand without, desiring to speak with thee.

But he answered and said unto him that told him, Who is my mother? and who are my brethren?

And he stretched forth his hand toward his disciples, and said, Behold my mother and my brethren!

For whosoever shall do the will of my Father which is in heaven, the same is my brother, and sister, and mother (Matt. 12:46-50).

Jesus is pointing beyond the biological family to another family—the family of the heart. All who are rightly related to him are related to each other in a new and wonderful way. The church has had a sense that there was a role to be fulfilled here. The early fathers used to say, "A man cannot have God for his father who does not have the church for his mother." Rather unfortunately they lacked the methods for putting this into practice.

Have you been to church lately? You might be surprised at what is going on there. Please don't just go to the Sunday morning worship service. Join a Sunday School class or a share group and enter into one of those situations that puts you close to other people. You stand a good chance of suddenly realizing how marvelous it is to belong to the wonderful family of God.

While conducting a conference in a church in the Carolinas, I suggested to the congregation that the time had come for us to put into practice the concept of NIEF. In Southern Baptist churches prospective new church members walk to the front of the church during the singing of the invitational hymn to indicate their desire for membership and the pastor presents them to the congregation, which votes them into the membership. My suggestion—when a new member is voted into fellowship the pastor should invite the church members to become the new intentional relatives, a father, a mother, brother, sister, cousin. This practice would fulfill a need in the lives of both the new and the old church members.

I made this suggestion at the Friday evening meeting. In the church service on the following Sunday morning at the time of invitation to membership, a family consisting of a father, mother, and two daughters came to the front of the church to indicate a desire to transfer their membership. After talking with them, the pastor announced to the congregation that the new members had a special need and asked the members of the church to commit themselves to pray for their new members.

No sooner were the words out of the pastor's mouth than a very attractive teenage girl came to the front of the church and put her arms around the girls. In quick succession there came other people until some fourteen or fifteen stood around them. Then spontaneously the group of people—new family and all—fell to their knees and began to pray for the new family members.

That family will never forget the Sunday that they joined the New Intentional Extended Family.

The concept of NIEF will not only help the family but will also bring the church into a new sense of mission. It will help the organized church to realize it is faced with some new opportunities. There have been periods of time when the church was able to supply a special need. There was the challenge of paganism in its early days which was met by the apostolic message of the gospel; the challenge of ignorance answered by the church's educational and teaching programs; the challenge of disease met with Christian hospitals; the debasement of child life responded to with Sunday Schools; the darkness of heathendom answered with missions. Now has come the challenge of the deteriorating and collapsing family and the church comes with NIEF, the New Intentional Extended Family. What other institution could meet these needs? There is no other existing agency under heaven that could so effectively minister to the family and it may be said of the church, as it was to Esther in the threatened extinction of her people, "Who knoweth whether thou art come to the kingdom for such a time as this?" (Esther 4:14).

11
Learn to Say No to No

Large corporations generally list themselves on the Stock Exchange with three-letter symbols that give some indication of the company name or the enterprise in which they are engaged. International Business Machines, for example, is listed as IBM, General Motors as GM, Goodyear Tires as GT, and Bethlehem Steel as BS. But when Combined International Corporation was officially listed on the New York Stock Exchange it used the apparently unrelated and rather unusual symbol of PMA. These letters, however, happened to represent the product upon which this enterprise has been built—a thought—a special kind of thought—the PMA, a Positive Mental Attitude.

The founder and inspirer of this insurance empire is W. Clements Stone, referred to as "Insurance Salesman Extra-ordinarie," whose assets in the holding company have been valued at an estimated $12 million and coolly states his objective, "All I want to do is change the world." Now seventy-eight years of age, Stone looks back on fifty-eight years of working in which he parlayed a business selling twenty-five-cents-a-week accident and health insurance poli-cies into an insurance empire and recalls his attitude in those beginning days, "I never doubted for a moment that I would be a great success."[1] Indicating what time has done to him, with a modicum of modesty, he surveys the world from the perspective of his seventy-eight years and says, "I'm happy, I'm healthy, I'm terrific."[2]

Stone's statement about the way in which his PMA has made him "happy and healthy" may remind us that a positive attitude affects our health and has a relation to the experience of stress. Stress is the result of a number of factors, a certain event that took place, the way in which the individual reacted to the event, and the steps taken in an effort to cope. Because of the wide variety of reactions, one researcher, Dr. Richard S. Lazarus,[3] began to question some widely held ideas about helping people under stress. In one paper, "The Power of Positive Thinking, Was Norman Vincent Peale Right?" he presents a convincing argument that denial, refusing to face facts, and illusion, taking some unorthodox attitudes towards reality, might provide the individual with some first-rate mechanisms for handling stress.

In the past it has been widely accepted that the outstanding indicator of mental health was what was often referred to as reality testing. This meant realistically facing the truth about a situation no matter how painful or upsetting it might be. The procedure was dramatized in the medical world where medical doctors had been accused of withholding information from a patient. The doctor was urged to tell the patient the whole truth.

In a situation where a doctor concluded a patient's condition was terminal, in keeping with the ethics of his profession and seeking to be honest and truthful, he informed the patient kindly and realistically about his condition. Two possible responses on the patient's part were possible. One was to stoically and bravely accept the news. The other was to refuse to face the reality, using the mechanisms of denial and illusion, seeking to avoid the horrendous message. One of the stated objectives of those who work with the dying has been to help them face the tendency to use denial and illusion as escape mechanisms and assist the terminally ill person to realistically face the situation that death is coming and must be honestly faced.

Joe Simpson was a case in point. He had lived a useful and fulfilling, active life. Then came some unusual pains. Being of a quiet disposition, Joe was loath to complain and his wife had to continually urge him to go to the doctor. At the doctor's office she had to push Joe to get him to describe the details of the pain he was experiencing. Joe was admitted to the hospital and underwent a series of tests. The results were not good. He had a malignancy, a type that developed very rapidly. The doctor informed Joe his condition was incurable. Joe was told that he could go home to spend his last days with his family and they decided to rent a hospital bed. As they talked with the rental agency representative, he asked how long they would need the bed, and Joe, recollecting what his doctor had said, replied, "We'll only need it for a month." Within a month Joe was dead.

Joe's experience raises at least one disquieting question. As commendable as the very fine and conscientious doctor's attitude might have been from some perspectives, was it redemptive or was it like a death sentence? Knowing the power of witch doctors in a primitive society, or placebos in medical experiments, could it be the medical man was unconsciously passing on a message that would mean the end of life for the patient. Was there another response that might have been effective such as, "It is very serious, the future doesn't look good, however, we do not know for certain; there is always a possibility for remission."

Whether illusion and denial are really as bad as they have

been made out to be now becomes a moot question. Lazarus's work has called this posture into question and suggested that both denial and illusion may have some positive values. He says, "My own research on how people actually deal with life crises has brought me around to the view that illusion and self-deception can have positive values in a person's psychological economy."[4]

Simonton and Creighton[5] have also produced evidence to show that reality testing may not be all that it is cracked up to be and may not be as realistic as some people imagine. These researchers discuss 159 patients diagnosed as "medically incurable malignancy" with a life expectancy of twelve months. Four years later they were able to report that following a special program, sixty-five of them were still alive. Of these, twenty-six either showed no evidence of the disease or that their tumors had regressed. If each of these patients had been pushed into "reality testing," the story might have been different, with all of them succumbing within the prescribed twelve-month period. When we remember that an essential feature of the Simonton regimen is for the patient to have a positive attitude, a strong desire to live, or an objective to move toward, perhaps he needs both denial and illusion.

We humans are so shortsighted. As a young man, I took a correspondence course in which an assignment called for me to write out my life goals. I hesitatingly put on paper a series of objectives which at the time seemed really audacious. Rereading them today I am amazed at my own myopia. Limited by the surroundings and circumstances of those days, I did not dare to envisage my real potential.

Too many of us are looking in the wrong direction and spend our days with our heads turned around, looking backward to the negative experiences of the past. When we

engage in these backward-looking practices, we miss out on
the possibilities of the present. Psychologists have not helped
us. Many of the psychoanalysts have emphasized such ideas
as, "The drama of life is but a repetition of the plot of
infancy," scaring us with such ideas as that the develop-
mental processes of personality are decided by the child's
fourth year, making the child indeed "father to the man,"
with yesterday's negative experiences continuing to influence
us throughout our days.

Other voices have been raised in more recent days. Psychiatrist Yalom says, "It may be the present affects the past
much more than the past affects the present."[6] Looking back
from the perspective of the present, we have a tendency to be
selective in focusing on the unfortunate events of our past
and of blaming these traumatic experiences for what is presently happening to us. Our negative expectations are all too
frequently fulfilled. If we expect to be emotionally crippled
by the past events of our life's experiences, there is a good
chance that's the way it will be. A positive strategy has possibilities. What if we sit down and review all the good things,
the positive things which have provided us with tremendous
potentialities for superior performances in life. Such an attitude can do as much to enrich as dwelling on the negative
past events did to impoverish us.

One of the negative emotional cripplers is resentment. It
not only fouls up the relationships of husbands and wives but
also becomes a deterrent to achieving our potential. The
essence of the problem of resentment is a negative attitude,
causing the subject to continually return mentally to some
earlier negative experiences in life. The word *resent* means
literally to feel back. The problem with resentment is that in
giving us emotional satisfaction from negative events which

took place in the past we foul up our present world.

The futility of looking back is seen in the person who has developed an interest in ham radio and discovers the biggest hurdle is learning the Morse code, which is really another language. The learner of Morse code looks toward the day when at the sound of dah-dit-dah-dah, the letter "y" will immediately spring to his mind, but rather unfortunately it doesn't always work like this and the temptation for the receiver who is listening to the code is to say to himself, "What is dah-dit-dah-dah?" While he continues to recall what this combination of dit's and dah's means, the other letters of the message continue to come to his ears and he misses them. The standard counsel to someone who is learning the Morse code is, "If you miss a letter, forget it." If the would-be receiver focuses on the earlier letters, he will miss the present.

This is the way resentment affects personality. The resentful person spends so much time recalling the past events that he misses out on the present. He is looking in the wrong direction, hounded by the memory of the negative experiences of former years. If he is to really achieve, he must set up some goals and expectations, unreal though they seem to be at the moment.

In the following chapter we will consider the imaging process and the way it can be utilized for healing. One technique of imaging is referred to as "directing the movies of your mind." Most of us are familiar with movies of our minds but for few of us are they pleasant. Very often what were the daydreams of childhood have become the nightmares of adult fears and apprehensions, and if we have movies in our minds they are of the genre of disaster or horror movies or at their best a series of disturbing flashbacks. These disasters, horrors, or flashbacks are negative.

The title of the book *Directing the Movies of Your Mind*[7] contains one very significant word, *directing*. As any movie buff will tell you, a director is just that. He does not allow the film crew or the cast to decide the way the filming of the movie will go. He is a tyrant, in absolute control and will ruthlessly edit the film in the cutting room, excising that which does not meet his approval. He will brook no interference. We noticed at the beginning of this chapter the way in which a noted psychologist raised the question, "Was Norman Vincent Peale Right?" It may be that if some of the positive thinking ideas promoted by Dr. Peale had had more of our attention we might have been much better off. Whatever critics may say, positive thinking means the subject is given a sense of control over the situation and a feeling that he or she can decide what way his or her thoughts are going to move.

A new executive had been hired and was being briefed by the company president. As they reviewed the various personalities presently directing the organization, they came to the name of the sales manager. The president repeated the name then said, "This man has a remarkable capacity for inspiring the salesmen and developing a positive attitude with them. You can move or replace any others but don't do anything to upset him, he is the one indispensable man." People who are positive, or are capable of producing a positive attitude in others, are so few as to be invaluable.

Any sales manager will attest to the motivational value of the widely circulated idea of PMA, a Positive Mental Attitude. These motivators will go to untold trouble to inculcate this positive attitude into the members of their sales force. Negative, self-effacing salesmen don't establish record sales.

If commercially motivated businessmen will go to so much trouble to keep their cash registers ringing, surely we should do something about developing a positive attitude within ourselves.

The program suggested by Bry and Bair in connection with *Directing the Movies of the Mind* calls for the rejection of all negative ideas. They note the persistence of negative feelings and suggests that the subject should learn to "Say no to your no." The last step in their program calls for a positive belief of which they say, "The positive belief serves to motorize the visualization." With some effort and a sense of being in charge, like the director, the movies of our mind can be changed from "R" to "X" to "G," and not only give us a sense of well-being but also motorize us into new and meaningful activity.

12
Engage in
Creative Imaging

The doctor, whose specialty was radiation oncology, was involved in his work of treating cancer. His patient, a man with throat cancer, had a grave prognosis, less than a 5 percent chance that he would survive for five years. The case was so serious that the conscientious doctor felt he could try some rather unorthodox approaches to treatment. Prominent in the method of treatment decided upon was the use of the human capacity to conjure up images.

The doctor encouraged his patient to learn to relax, a process in the course of which the patient visualized a quiet restful spot, the cancer which had invaded his body, and the way in which the treatment was affecting what the doctor taught the patient to refer to as "the confused cancer cells." The attacking white cells were to be seen as white dogs or sharks who could destroy the "confused cells." Later the patient was instructed to envisage the picture of the confused cells which had been destroyed as being "flushed away."

The patient did so well following his regular orthodox radiation therapy and his unorthodox relaxation and visualization procedures that he began to feel better. Delighted with his experience, the man applied the technique to other illnesses from which he had been suffering. He started with a painful arthritic condition and later a sexual problem he had faced for some years. In both instances the results were good.

The experience proved to be so helpful that it confirmed the growing conviction of the oncologist that mental imagery was an important motivational tool for recovering health and could easily be applied to other areas of need in the human personality. The treatment involves a series of steps in which the patient is told:

1. Find a quiet spot where you can sit without fear of interruption. Sit comfortably, with your feet on the floor.

2. Focus on the rhythm of your breathing. Concentrate on this.

3. Relax and recognize that you are in a quiet place. Visualize the tensions as knots or tourniquets. See them coming undone.

4. Systematically tense your muscles and release them as you are guided over your body.

5. Picture yourself in an ideal spot for relaxation. See all the scenery, hear the sounds, smell all the aromas. (This process continues for several minutes.)

6. Create a mental image of the ailment or the pain which is bothering you.

7. Visualize the treatments you are receiving and see them attacking the ailment or helping the body to heal itself.

8. Picture the body's healing powers at work overcoming the ailment.

9. See yourself strong, healthy, and free from pain.

10. Visualize yourself moving towards your goals in life.

11. See yourself going through this experience three times a day and the accessions of strength that come to you.

12. Gradually open your eyes and go back to your normal activities.

The story of the discovery and development of the procedures has been told in the book *Getting Well Again*[1] by

Simonton and Creighton. While majoring on cancer, but including other diseases as well, this book calls for the extensive use of imagery in helping people get their illnesses under control.

The arthritic patient is encouraged to visualize his joints, noting the irritation and the granules on their surfaces. He sees the white blood cells coming in, picking up the granules, and smoothing over the roughened surfaces.

An ulcer patient visualizes the crater-type sore in the lining of his stomach or his intestines and the raw soreness coming from it. He is encouraged to see the soothing effects of his diet and his medicine, then the image of the good healthy cells as they multiply, the white cells carrying on with their cleansing work, and the way in which they clear out the area. He is led to see himself free from pain and moving confidently into life.

When the problem is high blood pressure, the patient is helped to visualize his blood vessels as pipes and the way the muscles are tightening and narrowing the pipes so it is more difficult for the blood to get through, forcing the pressure of the blood higher and higher to reach its destination. He is led to see the work of the medication relaxing these muscles and the heart more easily pumping the blood through to its destination.

To the well-known idea of relaxation the visualization process has been added. The subject makes a mental picture of tension, seeing it as a knot which is tied, a tourniquet wound tight, a fist clenched tightly. In relaxation comes release. The knot comes untied, the tourniquet is released, the clenched fist relaxed and hanging loose.

In one of the most interesting applications of imaging, pain itself is given an image. The patient is encouraged to visualize his pain as a ball of some bright color. It can be whatever size the patient desires, tennis ball, grapefruit, or basketball. The patient is instructed to project the ball away from his body to mentally change its size, shape, and color. Gradually he comes to learn ways he can control it and imaging pain as a ball has played a large part in the process.

One aspect of this treatment which indicates the importance of the visualization process is the assignment required of the patients who are encouraged to take a piece of paper and a pencil and make a sketch of their mental imagery at the beginning of the program. At the end of three months they are encouraged to sketch their imagery once again. There is often quite a difference between the two sketches. Some criteria have been developed to help in visualizing both the disease and the healing process.

Because images mean different things to different people, the image should have a special personal meaning for the individual. One prominent doctor in this field likes to visualize the white cells as sharks. With my Australian background of man-eating sharks, the figure is rather overpowering and I find it difficult to see the shark as anything but a ferocious predator. One of the tasks in this technique is to discover the figure best suited to the individual's personal need.

In one of our tapes I suggested that the subject drop all cares. My statement was, "Imagine it is the end of the day and you are going to bed. Let all your cares fall from you like clothes that you drop on the floor." Later, after using the tape for a time of meditation, we were evaluating our responses. My wife expressed her misgivings, "I couldn't bear to think of those clothes falling on the floor. I wanted to pick them up." So, instead of relaxing, she was working hard picking up the clothes.

A man whose hobby is beekeeping has developed his own imagery. His main problem with his bees was an invasion of wax moths which threatened the life of his hive. He learned that if he put the hive container atop a strong hive, the aggressive bees would drive out the invaders. He got the most mileage out of visualizing his arthritis as wax moths and saw them on the screen of his mind being driven out by the bees.

The principles for the use of imagery begin to emerge as:

1. The imagery must be familiar to the subject to be effective.

2. Disease must be visualized as weak and confused. The images used should show disease as vulnerable to attack. Damaged organs must be seen as repairable.

3. The health-giving forces within the body should be portrayed as vast and strong. The white blood cells are often seen as knights in shining armor, white dogs, sharks, soldiers, or more powerful forces.

4. These health-giving forces are to be visualized as aggressive and ready to attack. They are so aggressive and strong that they will soon vanquish the disease.

Speaking of the beekeeper who envisioned his arthritis as being like wax moths brings to mind the wonderful work of these little insects as they build their comb in which they will rear their offspring and store their honey and pollen. Having provided the wax from their own bodies and masticated it thoroughly, they construct it into cells with paper-thin downward slanting walls. The hexagonal shape of these cells represents the most economical use of space and architects have frequently wondered at the skill of these little master comb builders.

From a most unlikely source comes another evaluation of the builder bees in comparison with a human architect, ''A bee puts to shame many an architect in the construction of his cells. But what distinguishes the worst architect from the best of bees is this, that the architect raises his structure in imagination before he erects it in reality." Karl Marx was guilty of colossal errors in his writing about men and economics but in this judgment he was correct. The superiority of man over insect or animal may reside in his capacity to use his imagination.

When I first read some of the literature highlighting the use of imagery in meditation and healing, I felt as if I were suddenly ushered back into the world of adventure literature. The healing forces which are set forth as opposing illness and the figures of speech present a drama not unlike my childhood world of cops and robbers, cowboys and Indians, Sweet Nell and the villainous mortgage holder, the jousting of knights in the lists, the adventures of Robin Hood against the avaricious sheriff of Nottingham. Reflecting the confusion many feel in reading today's literature, an actor recently said, "I like a story with a beginning, a middle, and an end, preferably in that order." He will find it here. The drama of the personification of forces within the human body is presented in the age-old theme song, right against wrong, with the optimistic belief that the forces of ill health which might be temporarily in control could be defeated and health will triumph over the invading forces of illness.

All this talk about imagery is readily understood by the reader of the Bible. The Bible is a book of imagery. The writers of many of the books use concrete pictorial literary methods. Some of the books of the Bible are a series of stories. Many of them are replete with elaborate symbols. Such books as the prophecies of Jeremiah, Ezekiel, and Daniel in the Old Testament, and the book of Revelation in the New Testament, come most readily to mind. They include such verbal pictures as Michael and his angels fighting the dragon, the angel swinging the sickle and cutting down the grapes to be placed in the winepress of God's wrath, riders clad in white robes upon a red horse, a pale horse, a white horse. People who are familiar with the Bible have an edge when it comes to studying verbal imagery.

Not only imagery, the Bible is a book of conflict between right and wrong, light and darkness, good and evil. It opens with the drama of the Creator and Satan and throughout its pages rages the conflict which finally ends in the last book of the Bible with the triumph of the Lord of hosts. Significantly for the health practitioner the Bible declares, "The last enemy that shall be destroyed is death" (1 Cor. 15:26).

The wide use of imagery and the theme of the conflict of good and evil prepares the Bible reader to be an excellent subject for the techniques advocated by the practitioners of meditation-relaxation therapy. Mrs. Jordan had lived an active life and was involved in most of the activities of her church. In her fiftieth year, she was hospitalized and her family was informed she had a malignancy and needed to immediately begin chemotherapy treatments. Once her treatment program was inaugurated she was introduced to the idea of relaxation and the use of imagery. She picked up the idea immediately. Asked what sort of imagery she would use in her meditation, she responded, "I will think about the malignant cells as being like the forces of the Midianites who invaded Israel, plundered the countryside, and seemed so powerful. I will think about the white cells in my body as being the soldiers of Gideon who surrounded the Midianites at night, each man bearing a trumpet and a clay pot containing a torch. Then I'll see them as blowing their trumpets, breaking their clay pots, and causing utter confusion among the enemy. Like the Midianites, those confused malignant cells are going to be defeated.''

Mrs. Jordan had a head start in her treatment program.

We have already mentioned a writer who has presented a concept that makes an application of the visualization process to all aspects of life, and sees the imaging capacity as a viable technique for use in both medicine and psychotherapy. The book is at the same time both irritating and stimulating. Irritating because it occasionally wanders off into some rather esoteric areas, but stimulating in that it opens up vistas of new experiences made possible by imaging. Titled *Directing the Movies of Your Mind,* the book presents a program of self-help which involves the use of the imagination to project a series of movies like scenes upon the screen of the mind and opens up some interesting possibilities in the use of the imagination.

As with most ideas, it is not new. William Shakespeare had a similar notion, tied to the media of his day, when he wrote, ''All the world's a stage, And all the men and women merely players.'' Bry's figure of speech of the movies adds another dimension. The whole cast of players on acetate is readily available to be presented at any given moment. It can be run, reversed, or rerun at any point in time. All of us need to find the ''open sesame'' that unlocks the doors of our imagination to bring the movies out and to give us the opportunity to direct them so that we might have the appropriate imaging experiences which can be so valuable for us.

Imaging may be a gift of God which humans lost as they became more sophisticated. Children have such vivid imaginations that the borderline between fact and fantasy is often loosely drawn. As a child I was much given to such flights of fantasy and can still remember the deserts that I explored, the mountains I climbed, the motivating speeches I delivered, the fighter aircraft I piloted, the infantry attacks I led against the forts. Later in life when I first began to preach, the warning of the homiletics professor was against a sermon which consisted of, "just a string of stories," but I discovered later that the only thing many people remembered about my carefully prepared, exegetically correct sermons was the illustrations. When Jesus, the greatest of all teachers, wanted to show the attitude of mind essential for entering into the Kingdom he said, "Whosoever shall not receive the kingdom of God as a little child, he shall not enter therein" (Mark 10:15). The capacity to dream, imagine, and visualize may play no small part in being childlike as Jesus wanted us to be.

13
Learn a
Relaxation Technique

The problem of stress is the response of the body's preparatory mechanisms to threat, a response which puts the whole functioning of the body onto a "war footing," so that the subject is ready to fight a battle, a battle that is never joined. In this stirred-up condition of being prepared, but never going into action, damage is done to the delicate organs of the body.

Faced with this situation the question that immediately arises is whether it might be possible to bring a message of peace, an ambassador who will demobilize all the forces standing in a state of readiness and have the body utilize many of its built-in forces and capacities in productive rather than destructive activities. The answer to the question is that there is such a message and such a mechanism. The opposite of tension is relaxation.

One of the best examples of the powers resident in the human body is seen in the most creative of all female experiences—that of giving birth. It has been demonstrated that when a woman is relaxed the experience can be much more easily handled. However, as medical science increased its knowledge women found themselves in antiseptic surroundings with hospital facilities and the instruments and paraphernalia of operating rooms readily accessible. Now has come a significant new approach and in some instances women are having their babies in the same setting as their great-grandmothers did, at home. These types of techniques are increasingly referred to as natural childbirth and at the heart of it all is a way of handling the "fight or flight" reaction by using methods of relaxation.

These relaxation techniques which are so significant in treating stress today represent a new interpretation of proceedings which have long been known to psychologists. In previous times the techniques were widely used in inducing a hypnotic state. It was postulated that when the subject went into a trance access was gained to the area of personality which is referred to as the unconscious. Hypnosis itself was seen as an evidence of the existence of this portion of personality.

Therapists and others who used hypnosis became aware of a side benefit of the procedure. Whether the trance was induced in an effort to discover the contents of the unconscious, to regress the subject to an earlier stage of his development, or plant some significant idea that would affect his future behavior, the major benefit often seemed to come from the method itself. Asked how he felt following a hypnotic trance, the subject would respond, "Relaxed. I am more relaxed than I have ever been." In clinical notes on the case the results of the trance were often noted as "euphoria." Whether the attempt to survey or manipulate or delve into the unconscious had been successful or not, the induction process itself had been of value.

By a strange turn of the wheel, the behavior shapers—the practitioners of behavior modification—came along with the assertion that there probably wasn't any such thing as an unconscious. Despite this stance they came to see the technique used for allegedly tapping the unconscious was of value in its own right. In their behavioral approach to people's anxieties and worries they frequently used a procedure called systematic desensitization which calls for the use of relaxation procedures akin to those used in hypnotic trance induction.

The relaxation technique was given a great impetus by the work of Jacobson of Chicago. Jacobson concluded that anxious people could be helped if they would learn to relax. He designed a system of skeletal muscle relaxation which involved a process of focusing on different parts of the body, one at a time, contracting and relaxing each of these. There were six series of exercises focusing on the arms, feet, chest, forehead, eyes, and organs of speech. In the process of contracting and relaxing fifteen muscle groups the subject reaped the benefits of relaxation.

Another relaxation technique which has re-emerged recently is the method of autogenic training. Autogenic training consists of six standard exercises which are in turn divided into six separate steps in which the subject focuses on various parts of the body. The first exercise creates the sensation of heaviness in the limbs; the second, sensations of warmth; the third, a reduction in the heart rate; the fourth, development of a smooth regular pattern of respiration; the fifth, sensation of warmth in the solar plexis; the sixth, a cooling of the forehead. These exercises are aimed at producing a deep relaxation.

The whole relaxation movement gained considerable momentum with the development of biofeedback machines. These machines take various forms but the one that is probably most frequently used for relaxation is designed for measuring the electrical discharge of muscular activity. One preferred way to do this is to attach electrodes to the forehead (frontalis muscles), and the machine measures the electrical activity of the muscle, indicating this on a meter or by a sound. The subject learns to relax by reducing the indicators displayed or given off by the machine.

The one person of recent days who has written with insight concerning relaxation is Dr. Herbert Benson. In *The Relaxation Response,* speaking about the problem of stress, Benson says, "When not used appropriately, which is most of the time, the fight or flight response repeatedly elicited may ultimately lead to the dire diseases of heart attack and stroke."[1] From considering this potentially dangerous mechanism in personality Benson goes on to ask a question, "If the fight or flight response resides within animals and humans is there an innate psychological response that is diametrically different?"[2] Benson enthusiastically answers his own question by stating that there is a mechanism within humans that can save them from overstress and Benson calls this the relaxation response. He sees this as a method in harmony with the teachings of Christianity.

The method may have some wide applications which include physiology as well as psychology. Some researchers in the field of cancer have concluded that the elimination of stress may be equally significant in facilitating the body development of defense mechanisms for coping with the disease. According to this line of reasoning we all have malignant cells functioning in our bodies which are kept in check by the immunilogical competence of our bodies. A simple statement of this situation would be, "We frequently develop cancer cells that do not go on to develop into clinical malignancy because the body's own defense mechanism [white blood cells] destroys the cancer cells prior to tumor development."[3] These immune forces which should be countering the potentially malignant cells have themselves been countered by stress and the major task is to reduce stress and turn loose the immune forces so they can do their work within the body.

It follows that if this immune response within the body is to be enhanced, a program which brings a reduction of stress will be necessary. One publication refers to the new possibility, "It has been reported that individuals who engage in regular relaxation procedure, with some form of meditation, are more able to effectively deal with stress to the extent that fewer physical illnesses occur."[4] The task then is to learn and apply a program of relaxation.

A blurb on the inside of Benson's book on the relaxation response gives an indication of other potentialities in learning to relax as it suggests ten things a relaxation technique might do for a person.

- Relieves fatigue and helps you cope with your anxieties.
- Relieves the stress that can lead to high blood pressure, hardening of the arteries, heart attack, and stroke.
- Reduces the tendency to smoke, drink, "turn on" with drugs.
- Can be used to help you sleep.
- Conserves the body's store of energy.
- Makes you more alert, so you can focus on what's really important.
- Reaffirms the value of meditation and prayer in daily life.
- Can be learned without classes and lectures, in your own home.
- Can be used anywhere, even on the way to work.
- Has no dangerous side effects.

The relaxation technique brings us back to the now widely accepted idea that in the feeling-action sequence, not only does feeling affect action but action can affect feeling. Some research has shown that when the subject imagines, recalls, or reflects on some activity he tenses his muscles as if he were having the experience, albeit to a lesser degree. Jacobson then develops a corollary, "If you relax these tensions, you cease to recall or reflect about the matter in question."

The statement, "It is much easier to act yourself into a new way of feeling than to feel yourself into a new way of acting," has some interesting applications even if the action is one of learning a technique of relaxing.

14
Try a Different Type
of Prayer

One of the concepts which has emerged in some of the newer methods of treating the whole individual is the concept sometimes referred to as, "The Inner Guide." Dr. Carl Jung and his followers have long been impressed with the rich content of what they call the unconscious and the way in which mental images are apparently of great influence in people's lives. In further development of the idea, the Inner Guide has been visualized in many different ways as a wise old man, a doctor, a friend, a religious figure. This Inner Guide becomes available to help the individual in a variety of ways.

For the Christian there is no problem here. The Bible teaches that God in the form of the Holy Spirit lives within the believer. Communicating with God should be a perfectly natural experience and the means of doing this is by the process Christians call prayer. Prayer is an experience which takes many different forms but for our discussion we will focus on three different types of prayer: prayer that affects God, prayer that affects others, and prayer that affects the individual who prays.

As a young minister in Australia, I was greatly impressed with a pastor who had spent many years in the ministry. On one occasion this veteran fell into conversation with an electrician who was installing some new lighting in the church. The minister asked the electrician if he were a Christian and the man responded that he wasn't and one of the reasons was that he didn't believe God answered prayer. The faithful minister proceeded to tell the electrician about Dr. Barnardo's Children's Home in England. Known as a "faith" enterprise the home did not solicit gifts but prayed for their needs. This conviction gave rise to an unusual situation one Easter.

On this particular morning the Children's Home had run out of food, but Dr. Barnardo assembled the children in the dining hall and prayed for God to provide their needs. As he finished praying there came a knock on the front door. A worker opened the door to find a boy from the bakery standing there. The boy explained they had been baking a batch of the Hot Cross buns that English people eat at Easter, but the buns had been burned whereupon the baker told the boy to take them over to the Dr. Barnardo Home, and here they were.

As the minister finished his story the electrician burst into tears and said, "Sir, I was that baker's boy."

Praying affects God. In some wonderful manner when an intercessor prays the way is open for God to perform certain acts. The Bible says, "The effectual fervent prayer of a righteous man availeth much" (Jas. 5:16), and goes on to tell of the way Elijah prayed and there was a drought. He prayed again and it rained.

A second effect of prayer is seen when we focus on another individual and pray for him and God does something for this person. Again in the Epistle of James, "Is any sick among you? let him call the elders of the church; and let them pray over him . . . and the prayer of faith shall save the sick" (5:14-15). This is the type of prayer we generally refer to as intercessory prayer and is probably the activity in which we most generally engage when we pray.

The third aspect of prayer is that the person who prays frequently discovers something happens to him. As he prays he himself is changed. This is the prayer of meditation which has been practiced by Christians across the ages. One example is seen in the prayer of the heart described by an unknown writer in the fourteenth century:

Sit down alone and in silence. Lower your head, shut your eyes, breathe out gently, and imagine yourself looking into your own heart. Carry your mind, i.e., your thoughts, from your head to your heart. As you breathe out, say "Lord Jesus Christ, have mercy on me," say it moving your lips gently, or simply say it in your mind. Try to put all other thoughts aside. Be calm, be patient, and repeat the process very frequently.

Practiced by the monks in their contemplative experiences, a prayer like this was considered to be the acme of the prayer experience. Christian history is replete with stories of transformation that took place within people as they prayed. The most intense type of praying in this manner was sometimes called the prayer of contemplation and brought about some remarkable changes. Francis of Assisi spent nights in contemplation and had the experience of the stigmata, the appearance of wounds on his hands, feet, and brow. This change within the individual who prays is the most readily observable of all the aspects of prayer.

This prayer of meditation brings us close to an insight into the way that prayer works in our minds and bodies. The Bible has much to say about this type of prayer and has a recurring message about meditation as it tells of the way in which sincere people took time to seek God. As they communed with him they discovered how God releases remarkable healing powers he has placed within our bodies.

This message of meditation finds one of the finest expressions in the prophecy of Isaiah. Chapter 40 is a magnificent prophetic poem which begins with the statement immortalized in Handel's *Messiah,* "Comfort ye, comfort ye my people, saith your God" (v. 1). Then follows a message of forgiveness to a discouraged people that tells of the might of an all powerful God and the way in which the Creator seeks to sustain his people.

He giveth power to the faint;
and to them that have no might he increaseth strength.
Even the youths shall faint and be weary,
and the young men shall utterly fall:
But they that wait upon the Lord shall renew their
strength;
they shall mount up with wings as eagles;
they shall run and not be weary;
they shall walk, and not faint (Isa. 40:29-31).

The words, spoken to Jewish exiles in Babylon many years ago assuring them of their God's power and promising that they would return to their home once again, provide material for a twentieth-century seeker for solace and renewed strength amid the difficulties and pressures of life.

A pastoral setting provides a gem of devotion for the serious meditator. Calling upon the close relationship between man and animal in the sheep-keeping practices of Israel, the psalmist writes:

The Lord is my shepherd; I shall not want.

He maketh me to lie down in green pastures:
He leadeth me beside the still waters.
He restoreth my soul:

He leadeth me in the paths of righteousness
for his name's sake.
Yea, though I walk through the valley of the
shadow of death,
I will fear no evil: for thou art with me;

Thy rod and thy staff they comfort me.
Thou preparest a table before me in the presence
of mine enemies:

Thou anointest my head with oil;
my cup runneth over.
Surely goodness and mercy shall follow me all the
days of my life: and I will dwell in the
house of the Lord for ever (Ps. 23:1-6).

This classic passage encompasses a wide variety of experiences in life, rest, restoration, guidance, comfort, strengthening, companionship, and the time-honored phrases of certainty and ultimate destiny.

The forty-sixth Psalm, a song that apparently came out of a miraculous national deliverance, became a meditation gem with phrases that inspire the meditation process.

God is our refuge and strength,
A very present help in trouble.
Therefore will not we fear . . .

Be still, and know that I am God . . .
The Lord of hosts is with us.

The God of Jacob is our refuge. Selah (vv. 1-2,10-11).

The Hebrew word translated *Be still* literally means "let your hands drop" or "give up fighting," an appropriate theme for meditation.

The book of Psalms was the worship handbook of the Jewish people. These psalms often tell of the experiences of worshipers seeking to commune with God.

As for me, I will call upon God;
and the Lord shall save me.
Evening, and morning, and at noon, will I pray, and cry
aloud:
and he shall hear my voice (55:16-17).

The indication is that there was a regular time scheduled when praying was to be done. Interestingly, meditators insist on regular schedules for their exercises.

However, it is in the life and teachings of Jesus that the meditation message blossoms into full flower and the Christian concept of prayer becomes fully clear. The ministry of Jesus began with an attitude of personal prayer. Of Jesus' baptism it was stated, "Jesus also being baptized and praying" (Luke 3:21). This attitude of prayer represents the theme of Jesus' life from that time on, which was spent in constant communion with his heavenly Father.

Once launched upon his ministry, Jesus embarked on a plan of meditation that caused him to spend the early hours of the morning in prayer and meditation, "And in the morning, rising up a great while before day, he went out, and departed into a solitary place, and there prayed" (Mark 1:35). This practice was later to become a more widely accepted pattern for meditation. The morning meditation is

BIBLE VERSES FOR MEDITATORS

The eternal God is thy refuge, and underneath are the everlasting arms. Deuteronomy 33:27

They that wait upon the Lord shall renew their strength; they shall mount up with wings as eagles; they shall run and not be weary; they shall walk, and not faint. Isaiah 40:31

The Lord is my shepherd; I shall not want. Psalm 23:1

I will fear no evil; for thou art with me; thy rod and thy staff they comfort me. Psalm 23:4

If God be for us, who can be against us? Romans 8:31

For I am persuaded, that neither death, nor life, nor angels, nor principalities, nor powers, nor things present, nor things to come, Nor height, nor depth, nor any other creature, shall be able to separate us from the love of God, which is in Christ Jesus. Romans 8:38-39

My God shall supply all your need according to his riches in glory by Christ Jesus. Philippians 4:19

I can do all things through Christ which strengtheneth me. Philippians 4:13

I have learned, in whatsoever state I am, therewith to be content. Philippians 4:11

Take therefore no thought for the morrow: for the morrow shall take thought for the things of itself. Sufficient unto the day is the evil thereof. Matthew 6:34

For God has not given us the spirit of fear; but of power, and of love, and of a sound mind. 2 Timothy 1:7

We know that all things work together for good to them that love God, to them who are the called according to his purpose. Romans 8:28

My grace is sufficient for thee: for my strength is made perfect in weakness. 2 Corinthians 12:9

When I am weak, then am I strong. 2 Corinthians 12:10

Like as a father pitieth his children, so the Lord pitieth them that fear him. Psalm 103:13

God is our refuge and strength, a very present help in trouble. Psalm 46:1

The Lord of hosts is with us; the God of Jacob is our refuge. Psalm 46:11

sometimes compared with the activity of the Israelites who had to gather the manna early in the day. Some meditators speak about giving the best part of the day to God.

Jesus didn't live his life in a backwater. His ministry was soon plunged into controversy and his antagonists were frequently the established religious leaders of his day. A focal point for criticism was the healing of a man on the sabbath. Hedged in with this hostility Jesus turned to his spiritual resources, "He went out into a mountain to pray, and continued all night in prayer to God" (Luke 6:12). The night of prayer proved so beneficial that he was ready to make the vital choice of the twelve disciples who were to be his inner circle through the years of his ministry.

After a difficult bone-wearying day in which he had performed the miracle of feeding the five thousand, Jesus withdrew and he "departed into a mountain to pray" (Mark 6:46). For him, meditation was the means of spiritual and physical renewal. These were not just the resort of someone seeking to escape a difficult situation. The experiences were part of an on-going style of life. So we are told, "He came out, and went, as he was wont, to the mount of Olives; . . . and prayed" (Luke 22:39,41). Note the phrase, "as he was wont." This was a regular practice in his life. Meditators frequently point out the importance of regular sessions.

As in his personal life so in his teaching. Jesus urged his followers to utilize a style of prayer similar to his own. "But thou, when thou prayest, enter into thy closet, and when thou hast shut thy door, pray to thy Father which is in secret; and thy Father which seeth in secret shall reward thee openly" (Matt. 6:6). This was a new way of praying in contrast to the formal ritualistic prayer of the religious leaders of that day.

The age-old practice of prayer is being rediscovered, this

time by people interested in the physical well-being of suffering humanity. A researcher working on the use of meditation wrote a letter of inquiry to Dr. Benson, the author of *The Relaxation Response.* In a generous response Dr. Benson stated, "Religion and medicine have been closely allied for millennia, and I think works such as yours will perhaps bring the two back together again." The chapter which follows is an effort to apply the method of prayer to the healing of both body and spirit.

15
Experience the Power of the Healing Thought

Our journey of investigation into the power of the healing thought has led us into some interesting bypaths. Preeminent is the impression that despite the remarkable advances of scientific medicine, for which we should all be eternally grateful, there is a growing awareness that there is another aspect of health which seems to have been given scant attention. Perhaps the very successes in developing technology, techniques, and drugs for healing the maladies of humans, has caught our attention and caused us to neglect the largely nonphysical, nonchemical methods of dealing with illness.

Looking over the field of what has come to be called holistic medicine, we become aware of a great variety of methods for combating illnesses. These include such matters as the reduction of stress, the examination of the benefits an illness may bring to the sufferer, the use of mental images, the significance of positive or negative attitudes, the reduction of resentment, the effects of fear, the change hope makes, the natural immune forces within the body and the nonphysical ways in which they can be blocked or released, the absence or presence of family support systems, the use of relaxation and breathing, the role of exercise, and the place of prayer and meditation. Most of these methods are nonphysical and all of them nonchemical.

A major problem is that many of these methods of therapy have not produced viable evidences of their validity. The medical community has been insistent that any claims for systems of therapy within its own ranks should be supported by verifiable evidence. Naturally, it feels it has the right to demand at least this much from people outside its ranks. Such evidence is not easy to produce. There are many intangibles that enter into a recovery from an illness and some of us have a feeling that in this situation there are times when, in Don Quixote's words, "Facts are the enemy of truth."

In answer, in part, to this challenge, a study was carried on at Southwestern Baptist Theological Seminary where one of the most ancient techniques of self-help, meditation, was combined with and contrasted to one of the most esoteric, biofeedback, in an effort to produce verifiable evidence of the value of prayer and meditation enhancing physical health. A researcher in the psychology department compared the merits of biofeedback and/or Christian meditation in reducing blood pressure. As subjects for this research, twenty men and women, all with elevated blood pressure, participated in this effort to produce some reliable evidence as to the validity of either or both of these methods.

Each of the twenty participants in the research program had two blood pressure readings taken initially. The subjects were then divided into four different groups, each using a distinctive treatment mode.

Group 1. The participants used biofeedback techniques and Christian meditation. It was hoped that by combining these two methods, the best of the old and the new, the benefits would be multiplied.

Group 2. People in this group specialized in using Christian meditation only.

Group 3. The hypertensives who constituted this group

concentrated on the use of biofeedback combined with a relaxation technique.

Group 4. The individuals in the fourth group did not participate in either the meditation group or use biofeedback. They became what is sometimes referred to as a control group.

Group 3, the biofeedback group, was involved in the use of an Autogen 1100, a myograph machine. Utilizing this machine the subjects had electrodes attached to muscles on the forehead known as the frontalis muscles. These muscles are considered by many to be a general barometer of muscle tension throughout the head, neck, and shoulders, and are seen to be useful for studying tension and anxiety. Tension in these muscles causes a movement of the meter on the machine, and generates a distinctive sound which increases in volume as the tension rises in the individual. By responding to this sound and the meter reading, the subject learns how to reduce tension. The method is often combined with relaxation experiences that are apparently more effective because of the feedback given by the machine. One added advantage with the biofeedback machine is the psychological effect of attaching electrodes, activating meters, and the emission of sounds. All of these tend to impress some people.

The meditation group, group 2, were taught to relax, breathe rhythmically, and adopt a positive attitude while listening to the prayer which is variously called the "Prayer of the Heart" or the "Prayer of Jesus" and has been used by Christian mystics across the centuries. The prayer is "Lord Jesus Christ have mercy upon me."

The members of groups 1, 2, and 3 came to the counseling center three days a week for a thirty-minute session for five successive weeks. At the end of the five-week period each subject's blood pressure was taken. This reading was compared with the original reading taken before entering the program in an effort to discover which of the techniques was the most effective in helping to reduce hypertension.

The results were interesting. The group that used biofeedback exclusively did not show as much improvement as was expected. There was some, but not enough to be statistically significant. For some strange reason the group that used both biofeedback and meditation did not show any noticeable change. It had been anticipated that these folk who apparently had "the best of both worlds" would have benefited more than the others, but this was not so.

The really exciting aspect of this research was the excellent results with group 2 whose members showed a statistically significant decrease in their systolic blood pressure (the upper figure in the reading), indicating that Christian meditation might be the most effective of these nondrug techniques.

While the results are not conclusive and the study had some weaknesses, even if meditation had not been superior to biofeedback, it would still be something of an achievement. One study carried out in another setting concluded that meditation and biofeedback were equally effective, but, as a commentator noted, "Since biofeedback requires elaborate instruments and meditation does not, it seems likely that the latter would be more widely used."

The wonder of all this is that the Christian community has been so slow to pick up on the potentialities available. A great number of churches have built-in situations that would make it a very simple matter to institute meditation regimens. Many such churches have a weekly meeting especially designated as a "prayer meeting." The disturbing aspect is that very little praying is done at these meetings. They are generally preaching services. When praying is the focus, it is almost exclusively the petitionary type of prayer in which the participants present an unending stream of requests to the Almighty. Altogether overlooked are the meditation aspects of prayer, with their tremendous potential for bringing strength, fortitude, and healing to the person who prays.

Setting Up Your Own Meditation Plan

After reading this evidence of the effectiveness of meditation as a means of coping with stress, you should be convinced about its value for spiritual and physical health, particularly if you are a Christian. You already believe in prayer and that God can help you, now you are confronted with the possibility that prayer is an experience in which you yourself may be changed. The change that takes place in your body can be particularly beneficial for your health. This is not the primary reason why you pray. It is one of the wonderful by-products that come to you when you are involved in an experience of praying.

Many readers are ready to agree with everything that has been said and will respond with a knowing smile and murmur such things as, "More things are wrought by prayer than this world dreams of." Despite this knowing attitude, these people are suffering with high blood pressure, and dozens of other stress-related illnesses that could be greatly assisted by the relaxation response if they were able to master the technique.

When I first came to the United States from my native Australia, I met a fine Christian couple who lived in Los Angeles. They kindly invited me to stay in their home and I gladly accepted their gracious hospitality. When it came time for me to move on, we had a touching farewell. The man handed me a signed, blank check. He told me they realized I didn't have much money and they wanted the check to be a cushion against adversity. If I needed money, I was to use the check. I never needed to use that check, but if I had fallen on hard times it would have been ridiculous not to use the check which could have saved me from difficulty.

God is like that with us. He has given us all kinds of gifts and wants us to have them. We will be foolish if we refuse to use them. One of these gifts is the capacity for meditation but unfortunately few of us use it. What follows is a simple, easily set up program of relaxation and meditation that can make all the difference to you.

The program of meditation that can be so effective in helping reduce your anxiety and teaching you how to cope with stress, while at the same time improving your physical health, involves five steps.

1. *Prepare a cassette tape.*

If you own a cassette recorder here is your opportunity to use it. If you don't own a recorder, borrow one. However, a recorder may be a good investment, they are very reasonable in price and you will find many uses for it.

Look into the Appendix of this book where you will find a script. Insert a C-60 (thirty minutes on each side) cassette into the recorder. Notice that before you record you must press the record button on the machine. Now read the first script. Do it from the beginning, starting with the words, "You are about to enter upon an experience. . . ." Notice it calls for twenty-second pauses all the way through. If you have a stopwatch that is fine, but any watch that can measure twenty seconds will do the job. The timing is not precise, somewhere close to twenty seconds will do. Once completed you should write the description of the tape on the label.

2. *Select a place for your meditation.*

Look around for a place where you will be safe from interruptions, preferably some spot that is quiet and conducive to the experience. As you will note on the tape, it is possible to have the experience in a noisy spot, surrounded by people or beset with the sound of traffic. However, all things being considered, the quieter the place the better will be the experience. If your situation is noisy, you can get an earphone for your cassette player and sit quietly in a corner while you play your tape.

3. *Establish a regular time.*

Decide on the best time for you. The program will take about twenty-five minutes, so plan accordingly. You can do it in the morning or in the evening. Some have arranged to do this instead of taking a coffee break and they call it a relaxation break. Others find the lunch hour a convenient time. The really serious minded have two relaxation sessions a day, one in the morning and one in the evening. Setting up a regular time will help to more firmly establish the practice.

4. *Make yourself comfortable.*

Because this is to be a relaxing experience you do not need to sit on a hard seat, one without a back, or one that is too high or too low. Some people become so relaxed when meditating that they start to slump. Consequently, you need a chair that will support you in the case of such a contingency.

Should you lie down? The obvious answer to the slumping problem is to stretch out on a comfortable bed. The main problem with this is that your body is programmed to believe that if you lie down it's time for a nap and you are liable to drift off to sleep.

Remember there are different levels of awareness. Sleeping and meditating are not at the same level. In meditating you are actually very much awake. You do not need to go to sleep. So, lying on the bed is probably not the best idea. Instead, find yourself a comfortable chair.

5. *Focus your attention.*

In meditating there are two conditions, a body condition and a mental condition. The body condition is complete relaxation and the program will lead you through successive steps until you reach this state.

The mental condition is concentration. You will pass through a series of stages of concentration on various objects until you are finally focusing on a passage or passages from the Bible. You should be able to concentrate on these which is one of the major reasons why you should not go to sleep.

6. *Maintain a passive attitude.*

Despite all that I have said about concentrating on one thought, you should not be worried if other thoughts come into your mind. This will probably happen, but you need not worry. You are to remain passive. Don't let any part of the process cause you to be anxious.

7. *Don't worry about the time.*

Some meditation experiences are anything but relaxing because the subject is continually worrying about the time and checking to see how long the session has been. If you record the cassette according to the directions, it should run about twenty-five minutes. Forget the clock, the tape will tell you when you've been relaxing for long enough.

8. *Keep a record of your experience.*

Use the form in the Appendix as a means of keeping a check on your meditation experiences. Keeping records is a vital part of the program and will help you to see what has been accomplished.

At the beginning of this book we noticed the power of a thought or an idea to influence people and motivate them into action. We have now come to a place where we are seeing the power of a thought to affect our bodies. It is literally a case of "As he thinketh in his heart, so he is" (Prov. 23:7).

The thought can be destructive or creative. Consider the possibility of a destructive thought as is seen in the experience of Helen Gastan.

Helen Gastan came from a good middle-class family which had inculcated into her the ideals of hard work and the necessity to succeed. Helen grew up being a tryer. Whatever she put her hand to she did it with a determination to be the best in that particular field. One day while in college she heard that a modeling agency would have representatives on campus interviewing girls interested in part-time, and full-time, well-paid modeling positions. Although Helen was no beauty queen she was attractive, had kept herself in good physical condition, and felt she might just have a chance.

At the interview Helen walked across the room, posed as instructed, and then was rather casually told she would hear from them if they could use her. Two weeks later, having heard nothing, Helen made a determined approach to the agency. A young man talked with her and explained that they had interviewed dozens of girls but only a few of them really had any potential. When Helen continued to press him as to why she was not selected, he walked over and picked up a large full-length picture of the slimmest girl Helen had ever seen and said, "That is the type of model we want, tall and slim. Take a look at yourself over here." He led Helen to the three-way mirror, "Now honestly Miss Gastan, you are much too heavy and just look at your legs, they are far too fat. The only hope for you to ever be considered as a model would be to lose at least twenty pounds. Of course, that would just be the beginning."

Helen maintained her composure, thanked the young man, and departed. Outwardly calm, she was inwardly humiliated and determined she would show the model agency, and anyone else who happened to be interested, just what she could do. She went on a rigid diet and became an expert in calorie counting as she began to shed what she considered unnecessary pounds.

A year later Helen was in the doctor's office. She had taken off twenty-six pounds, was painfully thin, and manifesting a number of physical symptoms. The doctor immediately recognized the symptoms and insisted that Helen's parents also come to see him. He discovered that Helen had not only put herself onto a starvation diet but was also involved in an intensive exercise program. She constantly talked about food but seldom ever ate. Sometimes she would excuse herself from the table and take her dessert with her, saying, "I'll eat it in my room." Later it was discovered that she had disposed of the food in various ways. She was also taking large doses of laxatives and when her parents had managed to pressure her into eating, she would suddenly run to the bathroom where she would induce vomiting.

Helen was an example of anorexia nervosa, a strange psychological disorder which amounts to self-starvation and in some cases may be fatal. Anorexics show the tremendous power of a thought. This single obsessive thought, "I must lose weight," can be self-destructive.

But there is also the therapeutic power of thought. The healing thought may bring you new accessions of health and strength such as you have never dreamed of before.

Now go to it. Prepare yourself for an experience that may change you mentally, spiritually, and physically. You'll be using a time-honored resource of the Christian faith which is nevertheless as up-to-date as today's newspaper.

Remember the supreme promise, "My God shall supply all your need according to his riches in glory by Christ Jesus" (Phil. 4:19).

Further Reading

Jeanne Achterberg, O. Carl Simonton, Stephanie Matthews-Simonton, *Stress, Psychological Factors and Cancer* (Fort Worth: New Medicine Press, 1976).

Karl Albrecht, *Stress and the Manager—Making It Work for You* (Englewood Cliffs: Prentice-Hall, Inc., 1979).

Adelaide Bry and Marjorie Bair, *Directing the Movies of Your Mind* (London: Harper & Row, 1978).

Peter Blythe, *Stress Disease: The Growing Plague* (New York: St. Martins Press, Inc., 1973).

John W. Drakeford, *Children of Doom* (Nashville: Broadman Press, 1972).

John W. Drakeford, *Psychology in Search of a Soul* (Nashville: Broadman Press, 1964).

Max L. Fienman and Josleen Wilson, *Live Longer—Control Your Blood Pressure* (New York: Coward, McCann and Geoghegan, Inc.).

James L. Fosshage and Paul Olsen, *Healing Implications for Psychotherapy* (New York: Human Sciences Press, 1978).

M. Friedman and R. H. Rosenman, *Type A Behavior and Your Heart* (New York: Delacorte Press, 1979).

Ronald J. Glasser, *The Body Is the Hero* (New York: Random House, 1976).

J. Goodfield, "Humanity in Science: A Perspective and Plea," *Science*, 1977, pp. 198,580-85.

Lawrence Galton, *The Silent Disease* (New York: Crown Publishers, 1973).

William Glasser, *Positive Addiction* (New York: Harper & Row, 1976).

Kenneth C. Hutchin, *Heart Disease and High Blood Pressure* (New York: ARC Books, Inc., 1964).

Edmund Jacobson, *You Must Relax* (New York: McGraw-Hill, 1962).

Kenneth Lamont, *Escape From Stress* (New York: G. P. Putnam's Sons, 1947).

James J. Lynch, *The Broken Heart, The Medical Consequences of Loneliness* (New York: Basic Books, Inc., 1977).

Shirley Motterlinde and Frank Finnerty, *High Blood Pressure* (New York: The David McKay Company, Inc., 1975).

Walter McQuade and Ann Aikman, *Stress* (New York: Ed Dutton & Co., Inc., 1974).

Kenneth R. Pelletier, *Mind As Healer, Mind As Slayer* (San Francisco: Delacorte Press, 1977).

Kenneth R. Pelletier, *Holistic Medicine—From Stress to Optimum Health* (New York: Human Sciences Press, 1979).

George Pickering, *Hypertension—Causes, Consequences and Management* (Edinburgh: Churchill Livingstone, 1974).

J. D. Ratcliff, *Your Body and How It Works* (New York: Delacorte Press, 1975).

Lawrence LeShan, *How to Meditate* (New York: Bantam Books, 1975).

N. Yoirish, *Curative Properties of Honey and Bee Venom* (San Francisco: New Glide Publications, 1977).

Notes

Introduction

1. K. Marx and F. Engels, *Manifesto of the Communist Party* (Moscow: Foreign Languages Publishing House, 1957), p. 112.

2. Kenneth R. Pelletier, *Holistic Medicine—From Stress to Optimum Health* (New York: Delacorte Press, 1979), p. 39.

3. Ibid., p. 63.

4. O. Carl Simonton, Stephanie Matthews-Simonton, James Creighton, *Getting Well Again* (New York: St. Martins Press, 1978), p. 117.

5. "The Hospital Addict," *Time,* September 24, 1979, p. 77.

6. Pelletier, p. 31.

7. Ibid., p. 13.

Chapter 1

1. *Saturday Review,* September 29, 1980, p. 31.

2. "How to Deal with Stress on the Job," *U.S. News & World Report,* March 13, 1978, p. 80.

3. "The Stressful Life in Peaceful New England," *Psychology Today,* June 1978.

4. Pelletier, p. 59.

Chapter 2

1. "Let Your Mind Wander," *The American Way,* October 1979, p. 24.

Chapter 4

1. M. Friedman and R. H. Rosenman, *Type A Behavior and Your Heart* (New York: Alfred A. Knopf, 1974), p. 56.

2. Ibid., p. 86.

3. Hans Selye, *Stress Without Distress* (New York: J. B. Lippincott & Company, 1974), p. 39.

4. *Psychology Today,* March 1978.

5. Karl Albrecht, *Stress and the Manager—Making It Work For You* (Englewood Cliffs, NJ: Prentice Hall, Inc., 1979), p. 55.

6. Ibid., p. 71.

7. T. H. Holmes and R. H. Rahe, "The Social Readjustment Scale," *Journal of Psychosomatic Research,* 1967, p. 213.

8. *Southwest Airlines Magazine,* October 1979, p. 48.

9. Laurence Cherry, "On the Real Benefits of Eustress," *Psychology Today,* March 1978, p. 60.

10. Ibid.

11. William Glasser, *Positive Addiction* (New York: Harper & Row, 1976), p. 93.

Chapter 5

1. "The Consequences of Stress," Health Learning Systems, Inc., 200 Broad Acres Drive, Bloomfield, New Jersey.

2. Lawrence Galton, *The Silent Disease* (New York: Crown Publishers, 1973), p. 45.

3. Max L. Fienman and Josleen Wilson, *Live Longer—Control Your Blood Pressure* (New York: Coward, McCann & Geoghegan, Inc.), p. 78.

4. Jeanne Achterberg, O. Carl Simonton, Stephanie Matthews-Simonton, *Stress, Psychological Factors and Cancer* (Fort Worth: New Medicine Press, 1976), p. 10.

Chapter 6

1. "The Born-Again Spleen," News from the World of Medicine, *Reader's Digest,* December 1978.

2. "At Your Finger Tips," News from the World of Medicine, *Reader's Digest,* January 1980, p. 62.

3. *Prevention,* April 1980, p. 59.

4. James L. Fosshage and Paul Olsen, *Healing Implications for Psychotherapy* (New York: Human Sciences Press, 1978), p. 284.

Chapter 7

1. "A Church That Would Not Die," *Time,* September 10, 1979, p. 48.

2. Leslie D. Weatherhead, *Psychology, Religion and Healing* (New York: Abingdon-Cokesbury Press, 1951).

3. Emile Coué and C. Harry Brooks, *Better and Better Every Day* (London: Unwin Books, nd).

4. Weatherhead, p. 134-35.

Chapter 8

1. "Stress: How It Can Hurt," *Newsweek,* April 21, 1980, p. 106.

2. "Tranquil Tales," *Time,* September 24, 1979, p. 78.

Chapter 9

1. Lawrence LeShan, *How to Meditate: A Guide to Self-Discovery* (New York: Bantam Books, 1974).

2. "Jogging for the Mind," *Time,* July 24, 1978, p. 42.

3. "A Patient Heals Himself," *Newsweek,* September 24, 1979, p. 98.

4. Daniel J. Leithauser, *Early Ambulation and Related Procedures in Surgical Management* (Springfield: Charles C. Thomas, 1946), p. 146.

5. Achterberg, Simonton and Simonton, p. 210.

Chapter 10

1. John W. Drakeford, *Children of Doom* (Nashville: Broadman Press, 1972).

2. James J. Lynch, *The Broken Heart—The Medical Consequences of Loneliness* (New York: Basic Books, 1977), p. 239.

3. Lynch, p. 81.

4. Amitai Etzioni, "The Family: Is It Obsolete?" *Readings in Marriage and Family* (Guildford, Connecticut: The Dushkin Publishing Group, 1978), p. 47.

5. Irving D. Yalom, *The Theory and Practice of Group Psychotherapy* (New York: Basic Books, Inc., 1970), p. 70-71.

Chapter 11

1. "The Power of P.M.A.," *Forbes,* June 23, 1980, p. 141.

2. Ibid., p. 140.

3. Daniel Coleman, "Positive Denial: The Case for Not Facing Reality," *Psychology Today,* November 1979, p. 44.

4. Coleman, p. 47.

5. Simonton and Creighton, p. 11.

6. Yalom, p. 122.

7. Adelaide Bry and Marjorie Bair, *Directing the Movies of Your Mind* (New York: Harper & Row, 1972).

Chapter 12
1. Simonton and Creighton.
2. N. Yoirish, *Curative Properties of Honey and Bee Venom* (San Francisco: New Glide Publications, 1978), p. 29.
3. Bry and Bair.

Chapter 13
1. Herbert Benson, *The Relaxation Response* (New York: Avon Books, 1975), p. 25.
2. Ibid.
3. Jeanne Achterberg, O. Carl Simonton, Stephanie Matthews-Simonton, *Stress, Psychological Factors and Cancer* (Fort Worth: Cancer Counseling and Research Center, 1976), p. 3.
4. Ibid., p. 4.

Chapter 15
1. James Hasset, "Teaching Yourself to Relax," *Psychology Today*, August 1978, p. 39.

Appendix

A Tape for Relaxation Therapy

You are about to enter upon an experience of relaxation and meditation. There are four requirements for a good experience.

(1) *A quiet environment.* The best location will be a spot where you will not be likely to be disturbed. This need not prevent the experience, you can be sitting on a bus, or in some crowded place, but it will be much more effective if you can be in a situation where you will not be disturbed.

(2) *A comfortable position.* Although you need a comfortable position you should not lie down because you will have a tendency to go to sleep. This is not your aim. Sleep is a different state from relaxation and not as desirable. So just make sure that you are in a place where you feel comfortable.

(3) *An object to dwell on.* As you progress through this experience you'll be led by my voice and your attention will be taken through a series of stages. Ultimately you will be guided to focus on a statement from the Bible. Follow naturally after this leading.

(4) *A passive attitude.* Although there will be a focal point for your thoughts it may be that your mind will wander. Don't worry about this. Remain passive. Just gently turn your mind back to my voice. You do not have to worry about your wandering mind. This is a relaxation program. Nothing

about it should worry you or raise your anxiety.

(20 seconds pause)

You do not need to worry about anything at this time. You are going to forget all about the things that have worried you, bothered you, or upset you.

(20 seconds pause)

Now close your eyes and think of some place where you have been that represents your ideal situation for physical and mental relaxation. If you cannot think of some place you have visited, then create in your mind the image of the ideal place you would like to be for a time of relaxation.

(20 seconds pause)

Let it be a quiet place, perhaps by the seashore where the waves are lazily rolling up on the sand, and the cool breeze is brushing your face, or in a mountain setting where you are looking out over a beautiful valley and everything looks calm and serene, or maybe in a grassy meadow, or even in your own backyard.

(20 seconds pause)

Now see yourself as actually being in your ideal place for relaxation. On the screen of your mind you are seeing all the colors, hearing the sounds, smelling the aromas. If it is a grassy field, you feel the lush grass beneath you, the warmth of the sun shining upon you, the smell of the new-mown hay, you hear the buzz of the bees, overhead you see the fluffy white cotton candy clouds as they drift lazily across the blue sky. Just feel yourself enjoying the soothing, quiet, refreshing environment.

(20 seconds pause)

Feel the restfulness, the calmness of your wonderful situation, and let your whole body and mind be renewed and refreshed.

(20 seconds pause)

Now focus your attention upon your breath. Breathe deeply and evenly, deeply and evenly, think of nothing but your breath as it flows in and out of your body.

(20 seconds pause)

Say to yourself, *I am relaxing, breathing smoothly and rhythmically, fresh oxygen flows into my body, I feel calm, renewed, and refreshed.*

(20 seconds pause)

The Bible says, "Be still, and know that I am God" (Ps. 46:10). "Be still" literally means, "let your hands drop," "give up fighting." That is what I want you to do. Quit struggling. Leave yourself in the hands of God. You don't need to struggle. He will do it for you. From this time on we will follow a program of being still and relaxing.

(20 seconds pause)

Now direct your attention to the muscles of your feet and ankles. Imagine the muscles are becoming very loose and relaxed. You can let the tension and tightness flow out of your body.

(20 seconds pause)

Now let the attention focus on the calves of your legs. Imagine that they are becoming very deeply relaxed.

(20 seconds pause)

Address your attention now to the muscles in your thighs. Let the muscles become deeply relaxed, just let go and let the muscles of your legs become completely relaxed.

(20 seconds pause)

Now address your attention to the muscles in your hips. Let the muscles become very relaxed.

(20 seconds pause)

As your hip muscles are becoming more and more relaxed

let your attention shift to the muscles in your abdomen and your lower back. Let the muscles become very relaxed, all the time breathing in peace and relaxation and breathing out tension, tightness, and anxiety.

(20 seconds pause)

Let your attention move to your chest muscles and the muscles in your upper back. Once again let those muscles become very relaxed. With each breath you are becoming very deeply relaxed.

(20 seconds pause)

Now take time to concentrate on the muscles in your arms and shoulders. Let your shoulder muscles relax, beginning with your upper arms and descending down through each finger in your hands. You are becoming very relaxed.

(20 seconds pause)

Focus on the muscles of your neck and the back of your head. Let your attention move over your scalp and to your face and let those muscles become very relaxed. Be sure to let the muscles around your eyes and your forehead become very relaxed.

(20 seconds pause)

Think of your muscles as being bound with a tourniquet. The tourniquet is holding your muscles tight. Release it. Feel all your muscles go loose.

(20 seconds pause)

You are now deeply relaxed—more deeply relaxed than you have been any time today.

(20 seconds pause)

Take just a moment to survey the muscles of your body, if you note any place where there is tightness, let the tightness flow out of your body with your next breath.

(20 seconds pause)

Concentrate upon the circulatory system of your body. See it as a pipeline carrying the life-giving blood to all the vital parts of your body. Envisage the Alaska pipeline as it comes across the snowy wastes, carrying the oil to the energy thirsty forty-eight states. See the maintenance men guarding those pipes and their precious contents, notice the way they work to make sure that the oil continues to flow on its way to the places where it is badly needed. Sense your blood moving through your circulatory system to every part of your body, bringing the life-giving oxygen and energy.

(20 seconds pause)

Continue to focus on your breath as it flows in and out. Remember that oxygen is bringing life to your bloodstream and your heart. The Bible refers to God's Spirit as the breath of God. Feel the breath of God's Spirit entering into your body.

(20 seconds pause)

We are now embarking on a program of Christian meditation. Our theme is taken from the prophecy of Isaiah, "They that wait upon the Lord shall renew their strength; they shall mount up with wings as eagles; they shall run and not be weary; they shall walk, and not faint" (Isa. 40:31).

(20 seconds pause)

We are now turning to a statement from the New Testament, "I can do all things through Christ which strengtheneth me" (Phil. 4:13).

(20 seconds pause)

Continue to breathe deeply and evenly. As you breathe in say within yourself, "I can do all things."

As you breathe out repeat, "through Christ which strengtheneth me."

(20 seconds pause)

Be calm, be patient, put all your thoughts aside and concentrate on: "I can do all things through Christ which strengtheneth me."
(20 seconds pause)

Don't let anything in your mind interrupt your focus on this statement: "I can do all things through Christ which strengtheneth me."
(20 seconds pause)

Continue to breathe deeply and evenly. "I can do all things through Christ which strengtheneth me."
(20 seconds pause)

Think again of your circulatory system. See your arteries and your veins as tubes carrying your blood to all parts of your body. See these tubes with clamps on them. The clamps are restricting the flow of the life-giving blood. Now visualize the clamps being released. Let them go—release them so your blood can flow without any restriction. The life-giving blood is flowing through your body.
(20 seconds pause)

Be aware of what you are thinking, all the time conscious of accessions of strength. "I can do all things through Christ which strengtheneth me."
(20 seconds pause)

Forget all the distractions that would turn your mind aside and repeat, "I can do all things through Christ which strengtheneth me."
(20 seconds pause)

If you feel you are becoming drowsy or your mind is racing turn it back and repeat, "I can do all things through Christ which strengtheneth me."
(20 seconds pause)

Envisage your circulatory system again. See it now like

irrigation channels leading all over your body. As the life-giving liquid flows across the desert, see your blood flowing into every part of your body.

(20 seconds pause)

Let all your cares drop from you like some clothing you removed and dropped to the floor and recall, "I can do all things through Christ which strengtheneth me."

(20 seconds pause)

Continue to breathe deeply and evenly. Deeply and evenly and repeat, "I can do all things through Christ which strengtheneth me."

(20 seconds pause)

Continue to see the blood flowing freely through your body without any restriction upon it as you grow more and more relaxed. Your blood is flowing through your circulatory system.

(20 seconds pause)

Now open your eyes. Rest quietly for a moment and then move into the joy of what awaits you in God's wonderful day.

THE MEDITATION-RELAXATION WEEKLY PROGRAM

NAME_____

DATE COMMENCED_____

	SUNDAY	MONDAY	TUESDAY	WEDNESDAY	THURSDAY	FRIDAY	SATURDAY	BLOOD PRESSURE READING
WEEK 1 Morning								
Evening								
WEEK 2 Morning								
Evening								
WEEK 3 Morning								
Evening								
WEEK 4 Morning								
Evening								
WEEK 5 Morning								
Evening								
WEEK 6 Morning								
Evening								

*Make a check mark (✓) in the appropriate place.